Friends' Way 2

Margaret Fell's journey

Martin Budgett
Jacquetta Megarry

Rucksack Readers

Friends Way 2: Margaret Fell's journey

First published 2023

Rucksack Readers, 6 Old Church Lane, Edinburgh EH15 3PX, UK

Phone   +44/0131 661 0262

Email: *info@rucsacs.com*

Website *www.rucsacs.com*

ISBN: 978-1-913817-07-7

British Library cataloguing in publication data: a catalogue record for this book is available from the British Library.

Designed in Scotland by Ian Clydesdale (ian@clydesdale.scot)

Printed on rainproof, biodegradable paper in the Czech Republic via Akcent Media of St Neots, UK

Publisher's note

You are responsible for your own safety when using the Way. The publisher cannot accept responsibility for ill-health or injury, however caused. Be prepared to summon help in an emergency: see *bit.ly/MR-emergency*

Following the effects of the global pandemic, nobody can predict which of the facilities shown on our mapping and listed on page 7 will survive beyond 2023. Check for yourself before relying on any.

This route was devised by Martin Budgett working from sources identified on page 70 and researched during 2022-23. Before setting off, you are advised to check for updates and diversions: *www.rucsacs.com/books/fw2.*

Feedback is welcome and will be rewarded

Readers are encouraged to send comments (on the route and/or the book) to **info@rucsacs.com**. All feedback will be acted upon, and anyone whose comments lead to changes will be entitled to claim a free copy of our next edition upon publication.

Contents

Foreword

The summer of 1652 saw the gathering together of the Quaker movement and the formation of a coherent and cohesive new and true 'church' labelled variously 'Children of the Light', 'Friends of the Truth' or, in scorn, 'Quakers'. Founder George Fox had travelled north from his home county of Leicestershire and on Pendle Hill had a vision of a 'great people to be gathered.' He found this great people at the Whit Hiring Fair in Sedbergh and a few weeks later he reached Ulverston and the home of Thomas and Margaret Fell.

It was a dramatic time for these outlaw and outcast Christians. Fox's journey towards Ulverston is symbolic of the journey the movement made towards success and stability: the end point of a personal journey became the start of a collective one. Key to this success was Margaret Fell who became one of the highly significant early Quaker leaders and 'mother' to the movement.

Thanks to this book, we can now easily retrace the steps of those spiritual pioneers and begin to better understand the geography and social history of the land they were travelling through. Nothing beats walking to be truly on and in the land and alongside its past. Walking, we can have a sense of both past and present, of what was and of what is. We can be fully present to those we meet as well as reflect on all the markers of history we inevitably come across along the way.

The Friends Way allows us to engage with Quaker history and with wider non-conformity in the north-west of England, as well as savouring the rugged beauty of Westmorland. I hope you enjoy this lovely book, and also that you take up the wonderful, timeless invitation it offers to walk the path that led to the consolidation of early Quakerism.

Ben Pink Dandelion
Professor of Quaker Studies, University of Birmingham

South over Morecambe Bay, with Hoad Hill

1 Planning

Our previous guidebook *Friends Way 1* covered a literal journey – George Fox's walk in northern England in 1652. By contrast, Margaret Fell's journey was metaphorical. As Thomas Fell's 18-year-old bride, she became mistress of Swarthmoor Hall and, later, mother to their eight surviving children. After her 'convincement' – her transforming conversion by Fox's visit in 1652 – she became a leader and organiser of Quakers.

Swarthmoor Hall, where she lived for 70 years, at first became the national headquarters of the movement, then, after the HQ moved to London, its main centre in the north. Swarthmoor hosted regular Meetings – including, from 1671, monthly Women's Meetings, of which Fell and her daughters were prominent leaders. She was an active Quaker for half a century, from 1652 until her death in 1702. Her personality, social position, education, courage and advocacy gave strength to the movement.

Margaret Fell's life and work place her firmly in the tradition of famous women who defied the social norms of their time to become leaders and influencers. For too long, Fell was not merely overshadowed by her famous second husband, she seemed almost invisible to Quaker historians – albeit recent scholars have redressed the balance somewhat. We devote this book to Margaret Fell's journey as a heartfelt tribute. For our short biography, see pages 16-20.

Some readers may already have read *Friends Way 1*, which covered part of George Fox's journey, and some may even have completed its itinerary. This walk is complementary to that journey, with the only overlap being the 9-mile Sedbergh Quaker Trail: see page 26. Readers coming new to *Friends Way* are advised to spend long enough in Sedbergh to complete that Trail. However both long walks can be completed in either order, ending at Sedbergh or starting there. We hope that this book, like its predecessor, will introduce some Quakers to long-distance walking and many long-distance walkers to Quakerism.

A note on terminology

The official name of the Quaker movement is now the Religious Society of Friends. Although *Quaker* was originally coined as a pejorative term, it is nowadays (and throughout this book) often used interchangeably with *Friend*. In general, Quakers are more likely to refer to each other as Friends, whilst non-Quakers are more likely to use the term Quakers for clarity in speech – because *friends* and *Friends* sound the same.

Swarthmoor Hall c. 1874 (engraving)

Best time of year and weather

Most people will plan to walk this Way in late spring, summer or early autumn. Birds are more active and visible during early spring and late autumn, and wildflowers are at their best in late spring and summer. June may feel especially appropriate given the timing of Margaret Fell's first encounter with George Fox and Quakerism in 1652. Accommodation will be more limited out of season, and post-pandemic it can be scarce and expensive at any time of year. Overall the best timing is likely to be anywhere from Easter to October.

In theory, of course, you could walk the Way at any time of year. It is mostly low-level, never venturing above an altitude of 229 m (752 ft) – on the shoulder of Warth Hill: see page 42. Winter walking will always involve short hours of daylight, greater chance of wet, windy weather and sodden ground in the offroad sections. It's wise to keep checking on the weather forecast during your walk: see page 71.

However, if you live locally and can go at short notice on a good forecast, you could enjoy any section of it on a crisp winter day, as long as you make the most of the daylight. Unless you are familiar with high latitude (about 54° N) you may not realise how short the days can become, with fewer than eight hours of daylight in late December. It's easy to check on sunrise and sunset times ahead of time: see page 71.

Which direction?

We describe the route generally westward from Sedbergh to Ulverston because we are following George Fox's journey – with some variations to take in facilities such as B&Bs. Reversing the direction would offer the advantage that on trend you'd be walking with the prevailing wind behind you. However we don't believe that this outweighs the role of Swarthmoor Hall as the fitting culmination of this walk. Our text instructions cover the westward direction only so, if reversing, you'd have to rely on our maps: it's harder than you may expect to follow directions 'in reverse'.

Table 1

	miles	km
Quaker Trail	9·4	15·1
Sedbergh		
	13·4	21·6
Crooklands		
	8·3	13·4
Kendal		
	13·9	22·4
Newby Bridge		
	13·4	21·6
Swarthmoor Hall		
Total excluding SQT	49	79
Total including SQT	*58*	*94*

How long will it take?

The overall distance including the Sedbergh Quaker Trail (SQT) is 58 miles/94 km, so much shorter than Friends Way 1, which is 71·4 miles including the SQT. The route is intended to be spread over six days, including a full day in Sedbergh for the SQT. However you can split the route differently to suit your fitness, travel arrangements and accommodation choices. The route is intended as a long and enjoyable walk, not as a test of endurance or speed. Read also page 10 for factors that will affect your average speed.

Distances are shown in Table 1, which has sections of notably unequal length. For example the distance from Crooklands to Kendal is only 8·3 miles (13·4 km) to allow time to explore Kendal: see page 49. And the Sedbergh Quaker Trail is only 9·4 miles, but there is so much Quaker heritage to see that it justifies an extra day in Sedbergh – at least for those who have not yet completed it.

Accommodation and refreshments

Many walkers seek a hot evening meal and a soft bed after a hard day's walking. With this in mind, we have split the route in the expectation that you will probably wish to overnight in each of Sedbergh, Crooklands, Kendal, Newby Bridge and Ulverston. Table 2 shows where you can find accommodation and refreshments, or at least where you could in 2023. The aftermath of the pandemic may mean that some options may have closed and may not reopen. Check carefully before making plans. As of 2023, the only relevant hostel was the independent Kendal Hostel (*kendalhostel.co.uk*).

Table 2 Facilities along the Way

	B&B, hotel	hostel	café, pub	shop	campsite
Sedbergh	✓		✓	✓	✓
Bramaskew Farm	✓				
Warth Hill					✓
Crooklands	✓			✓	✓
Kendal	✓	✓	✓	✓	
Underbarrow *			✓		
Crosthwaite	✓		✓		
Newby Bridge	✓		✓	✓	
Backbarrow	✓		✓		
Bouth	✓		✓		✓
Spark Bridge / Lowick Green			✓		
Ulverston	✓		✓	✓	✓
Swarthmoor Hall ✣			✓		

* about 1 km offroute   ✣ Due to reopen 2024: check website

Table 2 also shows where campsites are available. A tent that you carry is of course the ultimate low-cost accommodation, but camping along this route could be very challenging. Official campsites are sparse, and you would need to carry heavy loads to include sleeping equipment, cooking gear and food. Long-distance walking while doing self-supported camping demands considerable fitness and previous experience.

Refreshments are generally covered by the main overnight stops having at least one pub, café or take-away. If your dietary needs are specialist, or if you feel you need frequent snacks, carry your own supplies. However if you eat a hearty breakfast and a good evening meal you may need to carry little extra food. However, you should always carry plenty of drinking water for the day's walk, unless you rely on purifying tablets or filters.

Whitewater Hotel, Backbarrow

Navigation, waymarking and experience

The mapping in Part 3 is detailed (scale 1:35,000) and closely linked with the route description. If you follow directions carefully, navigation should be straightforward. Distances are shown by mileage markers that are cumulative from St Andrew's Church, Sedbergh. Each page also carries a pale grey km grid and north is always straight up the page. The key to map symbols and colours is inside the back cover.

As of 2023 the Friends Way had no dedicated waymarking, and although there are plenty of footpath signs you need to stay alert for which ones you are meant to be following. We offer detailed advice about when to follow the Dales Way, the Lancaster Canal Trail and the Cumbria Way. The photos above/below give you some idea of the variety of signs to look out for. But you also need to be vigilant about when to stop following certain signs. On occasions you have to look for an obscure arrow or detect which gate or stile to aim at, or try to follow a trod path over open hillside that has not recently been trodden.

If you have never attempted a long-distance walk before, we encourage you to obtain and study our *Notes for novices*: see page 71. We suggest that you don't go alone, especially not in winter or when poor visibility means that map and compass skills may be needed. Having said that, if you take time to prepare and plan your expedition, this could be a very suitable choice for your first long walk, especially if you can go with another walker.

People vary in their ability to navigate and also in their preferred methods. We offer information about maps on page 71 and explain about the very detailed online mapping as well as the printed sheets. In addition we offer a GPX route file which you can use with a GPS device or smartphone with a suitable app: see page 71. Even if you are an expert GPX user, we advise you to carry a compass and paper mapping as backup, either using this guidebook or sheet maps at larger scale.

North over Cartmel Sands to Canal Foot

Getting there and away

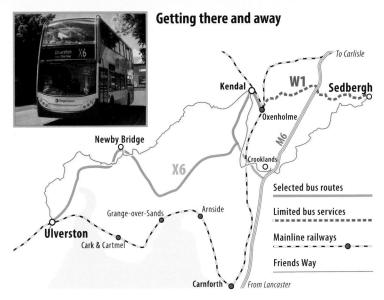

Map legend:
- Selected bus routes
- Limited bus services
- Mainline railways
- Friends Way

Map labels: To Carlisle, Kendal, W1, Sedbergh, Oxenholme, M6, Newby Bridge, Crooklands, X6, Grange-over-Sands, Arnside, Ulverston, Cark & Cartmel, Carnforth, From Lancaster

To reach Sedbergh, many people will use the nearest railway station – Oxenholme, 10 miles to the west. Woofs of Sedbergh operate a W1 bus from Oxenholme but currently only twice a day on weekdays, so a taxi would connect with trains much more flexibly. Oxenholme is on the west coast mainline and direct trains from London Euston take less than three hours (Avanti West Coast via Preston). To and from Glasgow Central, trains run via Carlisle and Penrith and can take as little as 2 hours with Avanti West Coast, slightly longer by Transpennine Express.

From Manchester, reach Oxenholme using the hourly train (Transpennine Express) for a fast and direct journey time of just 65-70 minutes. Northern Rail also has services, but they are less frequent, take a bit longer and you may have to change at Lancaster or Preston.

From Leeds, or anywhere on the scenic Settle/Carlisle line, trains run to the nearest station at Dent, from where limited bus services run into Sedbergh, so again a taxi would probably work out better.

To return from Ulverston you may find a train is fastest. There are trains to the West Coast mainline via Carnforth. Change for Lancaster to the south or go via Penrith and Carlisle to the north. If coming from afar, there is a train to Manchester airport. Alternatively, Stagecoach run an X6 bus service to Kendal (takes about an hour), from where Oxenholme is reached easily by taxi, on foot, or local bus service.

If you are seeking to complete this route in several trips, let alone as day-walks, be warned: rural public transport was both sparse and infrequent even before the pandemic and you would need to study the timetables carefully and check before relying on them.

Terrain and gradients

The Way runs over a wide variety of surfaces, ranging from grassy footpaths and farm tracks to stone steps, canal towpath and tarmac roads or pavements. The photos give some idea of the range, but rainfall (during your walk and also just before it) affects offroad surfaces and can make for slow going.

Some sections of the route have a number of gates and stiles, and you may be surprised by how much these small obstacles reduce your average speed. They present extra challenges if you are walking with a dog. Even flights of steps and footbridges may slow you more than you expect. Many of the paths are fairly well-drained, but you need waterproof footwear for walking in the rain and through long wet grass.

The route contains a few stiff climbs, all on good surfaces. They include the ascent to Greenholme (mile 4·2), out of Kendal (from mile 22), from the River Leven at Backbarrow (mile 37·1), from Bouth (mile 39·7) and the approach by road to Higher Lath Farm (mile 46·5).

How tiring a section feels often depends more on small undulations and the frequency of stiles or difficult gates, rather than its maximum height above sea level. However it's useful to be aware of the altitudes involved, especially if the weather forecast predicts low cloud. Navigation in poor visibility requires skill and experience with map and compass.

Your average speed depends on other factors, too: the Way features some historic jewels among its small churches. Many stand unlocked in daylight hours, and make rewarding visits, but you have to try the door to find out: even their websites are not 100% reliable about opening hours. Walking on tarmac is generally faster than on offroad surfaces, but take care on the winding narrow roads that are such a feature. Walk on the right to face oncoming traffic, but when approaching a blind bend move in from the edge to improve your sight lines. If the light is poor, be sure to wear bright colours or reflective strips.

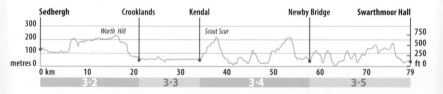

Responsible access

England has four categories of public rights of way: footpaths (walkers and wheelchairs/mobility scooters only), bridleways (walkers, cyclists, horseriders and wheelchairs/ mobility scooters) and two kinds of byway – restricted (no motor vehicles) or byway open to all traffic (BOAT).

Rights of way are marked on Ordnance Survey and other maps, and recent maps also show areas of Access Land that allow walkers to escape from paths under agreements reached with the landowners. Restrictions are explained at *www.openaccess.gov.uk*. In summary, in England you have no automatic right to walk over, let alone camp upon, privately owned land.

Countryside Code

Respect other people
- Consider the local community and other people enjoying the outdoors
- Park carefully so access to gateways and driveways is clear
- Leave gates and property as you find them
- Follow paths but give way to others where it's narrow

Protect the natural environment
- Leave no trace of your visit, take all your litter home
- Don't have BBQs or fires
- Keep dogs under effective control
- Dog poo – bag it and bin it –

Enjoy the outdoors
- Plan ahead, check what facilities are open, be prepared
- Follow advice and local signs and obey social distancing measures

Throughout this guidebook, we have been careful to direct you along footpaths, bridleways and Access Land. As you walk, be guided by the 2020 version of the Countryside Code.

Livestock, walkers and dogs

Much of the Way passes through farmland and moorland with livestock. There may be cattle or sheep grazing near the path or even standing or lying across it. Approach cattle with caution, especially if there are calves around. Most difficulties can be avoided by giving them a wide berth, staying alert to their body language and never approaching pregnant animals, let alone those with young.

If you walk with a dog, it must be under close control, and preferably on a lead. During lambing time (between March and June) your dog will be unwelcome in any fields with sheep. During the same season birds may be nesting on the ground, and again dogs must be under very close control. If cattle react aggressively to your dog, let go of it immediately and take the safest route out of the field.

Local words, placenames and pronunciation

barrow	large mound
beck	stream
dale	valley
fell	hill, high moor
gill/ghyll	ravine, mountain stream
ginnel	narrow passage between buildings
moor	upland, often heather-clad
rigg	ridge
scar	cliff

The pronunciation of some placenames may be unexpected and we have tried to indicate these below: place stress on the syllable in **bold**.

Broughton Beck	**brow**-ton beck
Bouth	bowth
Sedbergh	**sed**-ber (or, locally, **seb**-ber)
Staveley	**stay**-vlee

Packing checklist

What you need to bring with you depends both on your personal needs and also on your itinerary and the season and likely weather. If you are tackling the Way in sections, or if you have access to a support vehicle at any time, you may be able to carry few overnight things. If you are carrying everything for yourself, be aware that every kilogram counts. A heavy rucksack may weigh down your spirits, as well as making harder work out of ladder-stiles and steep slopes. Travel light and enjoy the walk.

Experienced walkers will already know what they habitually need, and may differ about what is essential and desirable. Novices may find the following checklist helpful:

Essential

- comfortable, waterproof walking boots
- specialist walking socks
- breathable clothing in layers
- waterproof jacket and over-trousers
- hat and gloves
- guidebook and compass
- in case of injury, whistle and torch for attracting attention
- water carrier and plenty of water (or purification tablets/filter)
- enough food to last between supply points
- first aid kit including blister treatment
- toiletries and overnight necessities
- insect repellent and sun protection (summer)
- rucksack (at least 30 litres)
- waterproof rucksack cover or liner, e.g. bin (garbage) bag.

Cash machines are sparse along the Way but cashless payment is widely accepted. Bin (garbage) bags have many uses e.g. store wet clothing or prevent hypothermia.

Desirable

- walking pole(s)
- binoculars: useful for navigation and spotting wildlife
- camera (ideally light and rugged), also spare batteries and memory cards
- pouch or secure pockets, to keep small items handy but safe
- gaiters (to keep mud and water out of boots)
- toilet tissue (biodegradable)
- small plastic bags for litter
- spare socks: changing socks at lunchtime can relieve damp feet
- spare shoes (e.g. trainers, crocs or sandals)
- GPS device or app on smartphone
- notebook and pen
- smartphone (cellphone): useful for arrangements **but don't rely on one for emergencies and have paper backup if using for navigation**.

Camping

If you are camping, you need much more gear, including tent, sleeping gear, camping stove, fuel, cooking utensils and food. Your rucksack will need to be larger e.g. 50-80 litres, and camping could add 5-10 kg to its weight. Previous experience is advisable.

2·1 Women in 17th century England

Religious dispute was a key feature of 17th century England. It lay behind the Civil War of 1642-49, the Glorious Revolution of 1688, the emergence of a hysterical fear of witchcraft and much else besides. Religion also determined the way women were regarded and the resulting constraints on their lives. In this case, however, there was not much dispute: orthodox opinion accepted the view that St Paul (or one of his followers) had set out in his Epistle to the Ephesians: 'Wives, submit yourselves unto your own husbands, as unto the Lord, for the husband is the head of the wife; even as Christ is the head of the church'.

As a result, the women of the time were second-class citizens. One contemporary claimed that women had 'no more soul than a goose'. They were born subject to the authority of their fathers. If they married, they became subject to their husbands. Women could not generally own or inherit property, and were themselves treated more akin to property. There were rules for them to follow in their personal conduct, particularly in relation to sex. A woman who had sex outside marriage was cast out of society and treated with contempt. The same did not apply to a man.

Not all women accepted such conditions. Lady Anne Clifford (1590-1676) lost her family estate after the death of her father in 1605. As a woman, she was deemed incapable of ensuring its upkeep. However, she pursued her case through the courts and, after nearly 40 years, she succeeded in winning the estate back. She spent the later years of her life restoring the castles of Appleby, Brough and Brougham, amply demonstrating her capability as as an estate manager.

Lady Anne Clifford

Women who spoke out against the patriarchal system ran great risks. It was common for such women to be expelled from their communities. More serious still was the threat of becoming the target of a witch hunt. There had been a fear of witches since ancient times, but it reached a peak in the 17th century. Persecutions had previously been rare. After the Reformation, witch hunts became more common. James I, King of England from 1603, wrote extensively on the subject and encouraged persecution.

Those tried for witchcraft were overwhelmingly women. The accused were denied lawyers and were not permitted to call witnesses. Torture was commonplace, and conviction and execution the most likely outcomes. In 1612 twelve people from the area around Pendle Hill were accused of ten murders using witchcraft, and nearly all were executed by hanging, including Alice Nutter – from a respectable, wealthy family. She was commemorated by a statue at Roughlee, Lancashire in 2012. In the later 17th century, however, the hysterical fear of witches began to die down. Three executions at Exeter in 1682 were the last in England. Much of the legislation remained in place, with the last Witchcraft Act being repealed only in 1951.

Statue of Alice Nutter, Roughlee

Poorer women often had low-paid jobs in spinning, weaving and associated trades, e.g. milliners, dyers and embroiderers. Many worked as washerwomen or as domestic servants, and some as brewers, bakers and confectioners. Some had the training to allow them to practise as midwives and apothecaries. A few women were even admitted to trade guilds as full members. The role of women expanded in providing care, especially to paupers. They operated nursing homes for the homeless and sick and looked after orphans and lunatics. After 1700 these roles declined with the spread of the system of parish workhouses.

Households tended to be largely self-sufficient, but maintaining them was very labour-intensive. In middle- and upper-class households, the wife was responsible for supervising servants, if any. She was expected to undertake or oversee domestic activities such as baking bread, brewing beer, salting meat and making pickles and preserves. Domestic work was dominated by chores like collecting and heating water, making and tending fires, preparing and cooking food, household cleaning and child care. Labour-saving devices were few, although the painting below shows a dog-powered treadmill turning the roasting spit.

Educational opportunities for girls had been extremely limited during the middle ages. However, the 17th century saw change: in some towns, girls could attend Dame schools. Some did little more than child-minding, but others would teach at least reading. Schools for better-off girls offered a more extensive curriculum but with a focus on genteel studies such as writing, music and needlework.

Religious study and even discussion was considered an acceptable activity for women who could read. Such study offered a context in which women could communicate ideas. Letter-writing and keeping diaries also enabled women to express themselves. The spread of literacy among women resulted in the publication in 1693 of the first women's magazine, *The Ladies Mercury*.

By the end of the century, the period of religious conflict which had begun with Luther's publication of his 95 theses in 1517 was ending. The 18th century saw extensive warfare, but its causes were generally not religious. Tolerance of different viewpoints was spreading Although women remained subordinate, a few remarkable females behaved with increasing independence. Change was in the air. A shining example was Margaret Fell, who became an equal partner with George Fox in the foundation of Quakerism, as the next section explains.

2·2 Margaret Fell and Quakerism

Margaret Fell's key role cannot be understood without reference to her second husband – George Fox (1624-91). Readers unfamiliar with Fox's story can refer to our five-page biography from Friends Way 1: see *bit.ly/RR-Fox*. Like Fox, Fell was imprisoned for her Quaker beliefs, and she used her time in prison to write and publish closely argued religious tracts and persuasive letters. She wasn't imprisoned as often as Fox, nor for nearly as long; whenever at liberty, she used her influence to promote Quakerism. She campaigned tirelessly for the release of many persecuted Quakers.

Margaret was, by the standards of the time, highly educated with a lively intellect, and she wrote extensively and persuasively. She was skilful at identifying abuses by the authorities when persecuting Quakers, including their use of warrants, searches, seizures, arrests and imprisonment. She clearly learned legal concepts, principles and practice during her 26-year marriage to Judge Fell.

In 17th century England, women's influence waxed and waned with their marital status. Fell was married twice – to Thomas Fell from 1632 until his death in 1658, and to George Fox from 1669 to 1691. Marriage to Fell made her the mistress of Swarthmoor Hall and enhanced her access to powerful people and increased her status. Much later, her position as George Fox's wife gave her influence among Quakers because of his standing. But during two long periods, she endured the marginalised status of widowhood.

Margaret's influence also was amplified through her seven adult daughters whom she energised and harnessed to the Quaker movement, which later also recruited their husbands. Her correspondence with her family was extensive and, with the exception of her son George, it seems that the whole family became a powerhouse of Quakerism. George Fell was generally hostile to George Fox, in contrast to his seven sisters who were convinced by Fox's message and affectionate towards their stepfather.

Mistress of Swarthmoor Hall, and 1652

Born as Margaret Askew in 1614 at Marsh Grange near Dalton, she was one of two daughters of John Askew – a well-respected member of the landed gentry, and grandson of the Protestant martyr and poet Anne Askew (c. 1521-46). Upon John Askew's death she inherited half of his considerable estate. At the age of 18, she married Thomas Fell (1598-1658) who was at different times a barrister, Judge of the Assize in the north-west, Justice of the Peace, member of the Long Parliament and, in his final four years, Chancellor of the Duchy of Lancaster. This arranged marriage was advantageous to both: together they enjoyed both increased monetary wealth and also social capital.

Thomas Fell was 18 years her senior, and his work often took him away for many weeks at a time. Meanwhile Margaret ran the household confidently and cared for the eight children they had that survived infancy. Thomas both allowed and encouraged her to exercise an unusual level of independence,

Margaret Fell's birthplace, Marsh Grange near Dalton

and Margaret received visitors even when he was not at home. When Fox arrived at Swarthmoor Hall in 1652, Thomas was away on the Welsh circuit.

Fired up by the success of his Whitsun Sermon on Firbank Fell, Fox had then preached in the chapel of Preston Patrick, in Kendal town hall and in Staveley – with mixed results. In Staveley the church warden John Knipe had incited his fellows to eject him and throw him over a wall into the graveyard: see page 59. After reaching Ulverston in late June, Fox heard of the hospitable household at Swarthmoor Hall and called there, speaking at first to Margaret's children (aged two to nineteen) and 'Priest' Lampitt (rector of Ulverston) – who clearly felt threatened by Fox and his message. In the evening Fox spoke with Margaret herself, and she reported being persuaded.

Fox stayed at Swarthmoor for some nights, and on 1 July attended Ulverston Parish Church at Margaret's invitation and (with Lampitt's reluctant permission) addressed the congregation. Margaret was deeply affected by his words, and defended George against Lampitt's increasing anger. After George was ejected, he addressed the crowd in the churchyard before returning to Swarthmoor and convincing most of the household. Margaret was by now facing a dilemma: 'I was struck into such a sadness, I knew not what to do, my husband being from home. I saw it was the truth, and I could not deny it'.

In early July, Fox made a series of journeys on horseback to preach and gather support in various villages within easy reach of Swarthmoor. He also returned to Kendal and Sedbergh to fortify his recent converts. Meanwhile Margaret and her household had their Quaker beliefs reinforced by leading Quakers James Nayler and Richard Farnsworth, who had followed Fox to Swarthmoor and been invited to stay on. Three weeks after first meeting Fox, Margaret sent word that Judge Fell was expected to return and beseeched Fox to return from Sedbergh.

Even as Fell was crossing the sands of Morecambe Bay on his return, a group of angry gentlemen led by Lampitt intercepted him to speak of the 'disaster' they had observed at Swarthmoor, claiming that his wife, children and household had been bewitched by a travelling preacher.

The accusation of witchcraft was very serious at the time. Happily for Margaret, Fell suspended judgement until he had heard both sides. After supper, Fell agreed to Margaret's request that Fox should speak directly. According to Margaret 'And so my husband came to see clearly the truth of what he spoke, and was very quiet that night, said no more, and went to bed'.

The next day Lampitt visited and in long earnest talks tried to change Fell's mind, but without success. When later some Friends were discussing the problem of where they could meet to worship as they preferred, Fell overheard them and offered 'You may meet here, if you will'. Two days later the first Meeting was held in Swarthmoor's large hall, and they continued on every Sunday until 1690, when Fox created a Meetinghouse nearby: see page 69.

Although Fell was clearly sympathetic to Quakerism and never hindered his wife's activities, his public position prevented him from being publicly identified as a Quaker. He continued to attend Lampitt's church without his wife and family for a year or two, maintaining outward religious appearances. In his later years, however, he would sit in his study with its doors open to the large hall while the Meeting was in progress – a discreet form of attendance. He was also a valuable defender of Quaker liberty and source of legal advice.

In the years following her 'convincement', Margaret took to writing letters, tracts, and a total of 16 books, four of which were translated into Dutch, Hebrew or Latin. Her subjects ranged widely – from freedom of conscience in worship, to the equality of women, a mission to the Jews and pacifism.

THOMAS FELL OF SWARTHMOOR HALL ULVERSTON, B.1598, M.1652, D.1658			MARGARET ASKEW B.1614, D.1702			GEORGE FOX B.1624, M.1669, D.1691	
MARGARET B.1633, D.1706	BRIDGET B.1635, D.1663	ISABEL B.1637, D.1704	GEORGE B.1638, D.1670	SARAH B.1642, D.1714	MARY B.1647, D.1720	SUSANNAH B.1650, D.1710	RACHEL B.1653, D.1732

All of Margaret's children married and about 24 of her grandchildren survived infancy.

Widowhood and imprisonment

In 1658 Thomas died and Margaret continued her work for the Quaker cause. Freed of any restraining influence, she acquired more autonomy in word and deed, as well as inheriting his considerable estate including sole ownership of Swarthmoor Hall. However she also became more vulnerable – no longer protected as a judge's wife. Nevertheless she was quick to turn her influence and eloquent writings to the defence of other vulnerable Quakers.

Another important death in 1658 was that of Oliver Cromwell who had established the Protectorate after the beheading of Charles I in 1649. Within two years of Cromwell's death, the succession struggle ended the Protectorate, and England's monarchy was restored. Charles II went on to reign from 1660 to 1685. Margaret began what became a long correspondence and series of visits with King Charles, spending 18 months in London on Quaker business from 1660. Her first goal was to plead with him for George Fox's release from prison.

During the summer months of 1663 Fell and most of her daughters made a 1000-mile journey all over England to visit and encourage Friends. The following year she was arrested for failing to take an oath and for allowing Meetings to be held in her home. Defending herself, she said 'as long as the Lord blessed her with a home, she would worship him in it'. After six months in Lancaster Gaol, she was sentenced to life imprisonment and forfeiture of all her property – Draconian punishment for religious belief and practice.

In fact she was released in June 1668, having used over four years in gaol to write religious tracts including *Women's Speaking Justified* – a scripture-based argument for women's ministry. This developed Fox's assertion that the spirit of Christ lives in both men and women equally and therefore each gender is entitled to speak and be heard. By 1667 it had run to a second edition which included replies to questions and criticism, and is considered a major text on women's religious leadership in the 17th century.

After her release from Lancaster Gaol and the restoration of her estate in 1668, Fell began to establish Women's Meetings in parallel to the existing Men's meetings. At first these tended to focus on issues around marriage, orphans and the elderly, and also about the employment and apprenticehsip of young women Friends. From 1671 she held monthly Women's Meetings at Swarthmoor, where she and her daughters were prominent leaders

Marriage to George Fox

Margaret's marriage to George Fox took place in Bristol, in October 1669. This may have been more of a strategic and theological alliance than a love match or a physical union. Margaret was 55 and had been widowed for 11 years, whereas George was a bachelor of 45. Since their first meeting in 1652, they had enjoyed many years of close friendship and deep mutual respect.

They married only after extensive discussion with fellow Quakers, whose concern to avoid any appearance of impropriety or scandal may have been a factor. Margaret's children were also consulted and all her daughters were supportive of the marriage. Once married, their separate Quaker work seemed to take precedence over spending time together. Just 10 days after the wedding, they left Bristol together, but George 'passed on ... in the work of the Lord into Wiltshire' while his bride travelled on alone to Swarthmoor.

Only six months later, Margaret was imprisoned in Lancaster for about a year for breaking the Conventicle Act by allowing Meetings at Swarthmoor. Shortly after her release, George Fox left for America on another Quaker mission, and he was imprisoned again on his return in 1673. Margaret went to London to plead for his release, and George was eventually freed in 1675. After this, they spent about a year together at Swarthmoor, collaborating on Quaker work. The companionable interlude did not last long, and in a rare moment of emotional appeal, Margaret's letter of 18 July 1678 shows how much they all miss him: 'Thy company would be more and better to us than all the world or than all the earth can afford; but only for the Lord's truth and service [are we willing to resign it]'. Two months later, Fox returned to Swarthmoor for 18 months.

By 1680, Quaker membership had grown to a peak and the establishment responded to their rising power by increasing the persecution. Fines were widespread and Quakers were often imprisoned. Margaret was fined heavily and had her cattle confiscated. In 1684 Margaret, now 70, made another journey to London to petition the new King, James II, but he dismissed her with a curt 'go home'. The Glorious Revolution of 1688 put William and Mary of Orange jointly on the throne, and the Act of Toleration was finally passed in 1689. At long last, the persecution of Quakers became illegal; both Margaret and George must have rejoiced at this achievement.

Over the 22 years of their marriage, George had been with Margaret at Swarthmoor Hall for a total of less than five, usually only for convalescence from his spells of brutal imprisonment. Margaret calmly accepted George's prolonged absences both in prison and on preaching missions. She often made the arduous journey to London, where George spent most of his last decade, staying in the homes of Margaret's married daughters near London. She was 77 when she went there in 1690 for several months, perhaps aware that he had not long to live. In January 1691, George Fox died in London and Margaret spent her remaining 11 years at Swarthmoor.

In April 1702 Margaret Fell Fox died serenely at the remarkable age of 88 years. Just before she died, she said to her youngest daughter Rachel 'Take me in thy arms ... I am in peace'. Her body lies at Sunbrick Burial Ground on Birkrigg Common. Swarthmoor Hall had been her home for 70 years, and it continues to inspire the Quaker movement to this day. And so does Margaret Fell, who lives on through her publications, which in 1712 were edited and published by her daughters and sons-in-law.

Wall plaque at Sunbrick Burial Ground

2·3 Habitats and wildlife

The Way begins within the Yorkshire Dales National Park at Sedbergh, but soon leaves it to cross the M6. South-west of Kendal at mile 23 it enters the Lake District National Park – England's largest, and a UNESCO World Heritage Site – and remains inside it until well beyond Newby Bridge.

Damson blossom

So this route features two of England's most popular National Parks, designated for their natural beauty, diversity of habitats and rich heritage. You'll find rich resources about each on their respective websites: see page 70.

To understand the different habitats that you walk through, it helps to know the basics of the underlying geology. Put simply, the walk runs mainly over slates, shales and sandstones formed in layers in an ancient tropical sea and dating from the Silurian period about 420 to 400 million years ago (MYA). The pale grey carboniferous limestones are more recent, about 380 to 350 MYA. They were formed by the deposit and compression of masses of corals and broken shells of marine animals. Modern fossil finds among limestone, eons later, show that the occasional shell survived intact. Although limestone is a hard rock, over time it gradually dissolves in rainwater (a very weak form of carbonic acid) and creates features such as caves, dry valleys and limestone pavement.

Two distinctive outcrops of limestone that you'll see are Scout Scar (whose shoulder you cross from miles 23 to 25) and Whitbarrow National Nature Reserve (whose edge you go around between miles 28·5 and 29·5). People used limestone in the past for building and they also burned it in lime kilns to create agricultural fertiliser. Happily, it is now protected by law. The Whitbarrow NNR is rich in butterflies, wildflowers and celebrated for its biodiversity.

From 2 MYA to about 10,000 years ago, the glaciers of various Ice Ages advanced and retreated, changing the landscape on their way. Throughout the latest one, a huge thick sheet of ice covered and pressed down upon the whole of northern England. When the glaciers retreated, they scoured out U-shaped valleys, deposited huge boulders called glacial erratics and changed the scenery again.

Whitbarrow from the Lyth Valley

Main habitat types on the Way

Excluding the limestone outcrops. there are three main habitat types:

- **waterside**
- **woodland**
- **moor and grassland**

Waterside

Grey wagtail

The Way traverses an area known for its rainfall and its many rivers. You walk beside and cross many streams (becks) and larger rivers include the Rawthey, Lune, Kent, Gilpin, Winster, Leven, Rusland Pool and Crake. The Way also joins the Lancaster Canal towpath for a couple of miles before it becomes dry.

Rivers and becks make homes and provide food for insects, birds and small mammals, as well as acting as wildlife corridors. The larger rivers are home to a wide range of fish including trout. Various kinds of wagtail make distinctive bobbing movements – especially the pied (black-and-white) and the less common grey wagtail, with its lemon yellow underparts.

Look out for the charming dipper, a small dark-brown bird with a dapper white breast, skilful at collecting larvae and insects from fast-moving streams. If you glimpse the turquoise flash of a low-flying tiny bird above a stream, it's a kingfisher. They prey on aquatic insects and small fish, and are a sign of a high-quality watercourse.

Sheltered between Scout Scar and Whitbarrow lies the flat-bottomed valley of the Rivers Pool and Gilpin. The Lyth Valley's microclimate favours damson orchards, especially on its western slopes. The late Alfred Wainwright referred to damson blossom when praising the 'supreme joy of the Lyth valley is its annual springtime renewal'. And its small plums are said to have a unique flavour, celebrated by the Westmorland Damson Association. The Lyth valley was formerly marshland where peat was harvested, and has been artifically drained since 1815 to make it viable for farming. Before humans intervened with drainage, it hosted larger breeding colonies of wading birds, and where small areas have been re-wetted recently, these species have recovered well. With the costs of the pumping and sea levels both rising, eventually the valley floor may return to marsh.

Oystercatchers foraging on tidal sands

On the western part of the Way you are never far from the coast and Morecambe Bay is one of Europe's most important places for migrating and over-wintering birds. Its vast expanses of tidal mudflats and sands are packed with cockles, mussels, shrimps and lugworms. It makes a huge feeding ground for many kinds of wading birds, including oystercatchers, curlews, redshanks and sandpipers. The differing lengths and shapes of their beaks allow them to coexist while finding plentiful food at different levels within the mud.

Woodland

The Way passes through mixed woodlands, many of which have been harvested for timber in the past or coppiced for the production of charcoal. Modern plantations mostly date from the 20th century, and tend to be dense coniferous forests, including non-native spruce, firs and larch. The poet Wordsworth devoted a whole page of his 1810 guidebook to the Lakeland Fells to a diatribe against larch trees. Unlike most conifers, they are deciduous and in spring their needles emerge afresh in a bright green, contrasting with the new cones, pink at first – colours that Wordsworth deplored.

Even dense forests are not devoid of wildlife: large birds need large trees to nest in, especially birds of prey. You are likely to hear the mewing of buzzards over woodland and hillside, and may see them soaring above, their wings held in a shallow Vee. Roe deer graze near the forest edges, especially near dawn and dusk; they retreat to take cover when disturbed. In spring, the woodland may be carpeted in bluebells, and may ring with the persistent call of the cuckoo. Deciduous woodland favours some colourful birds, including the great spotted woodpecker, which you may hear drumming on tree trunks, the dapper bullfinch and the tiny goldcrest.

The Lake District is one of England's last refuges for red squirrels, which have larger strongholds in parts of Wales and Scotland. Elsewhere they have been displaced by their American cousins, the grey squirrel, which not only out-competes them for food, but also carries the squirrelpox disease that is fatal to reds.

Red squirrel

Larch needles and cones in spring

Pine marten

Thanks to the efforts of various groups including the Cumbria Wildlife Trust and Northern Red Squirrels, their presence in Cumbria is well documented and monitored. And the reds may receive help from an unexpected quarter – an arboreal predator from the weasel family.

Pine martens once thrived across Cumbria, as many of its placenames confirm. By 1915, they had been hunted to the brink of extinction across most of England. In recent years, however, a few pine martens have been sighted and if they can establish a breeding population, it will greatly help the red squirrels. The pine marten is the only mammal agile enough to catch a squirrel, and they are very successful with the heavier greys. The lighter reds can escape pursuit by taking to thin tree branches that won't bear the pine marten's weight.

Moor and grassland

Moorland is very important for ground-nesting birds such as red grouse, stonechats, lapwings and short-eared owls. The months of April and May are crucial for nesting and rearing young: disturbance caused by people walking off-path or, worse still, allowing dogs to run free, can have fatal results.

The UK is internationally important for curlews, Europe's largest wading bird. About 30% of Western Europe's population over-winter here. The recent decline in numbers is worrying and in 2015 curlews were added to the Red list, with only about 58,500 breeding pairs. Curlews feed on worms, shellfish and shrimps, using their distinctive long curved beaks. In winter, they congregate on the mudflats of Morecambe Bay and other tidal sands, whilst in the breeding season (April to June) they nest in scrapes on the moors. Their streaky plumage helps to camouflage them while brooding on their nests, but they suffer predation, especially from foxes. If you hear a rising, burbling call like like an old-fashioned whistling kettle, that is a curlew – the evocative cry of the wild lonely places.

Curlew

Herdwick high on the fells

Open fellside has been developed over many centuries as rough grazing for sheep, particularly Herdwicks. Their name comes from the Norse word *herdvyck* meaning sheep pasture, and these animals are descended from hardy sheep brought here by the Vikings. They are 'hefted' on the land, meaning they remember their pastures and generations of Herdwicks will remain in place without any need for fences. They are agile as well as hardy and may be found high on the fells.

Of even more ancient origin than Herdwick sheep are the fell ponies that you may see foraging on high ground. These semi-wild ponies are extremely hardy, and can survive harsh winters by scraping the snow with their hooves to feed on grasses and mosses beneath. Their stocky build, shaggy coats and long manes sweeping over their faces all help them to stay warm. Although they come in various colours, the most typical is dark brown to black, tinged with russet. They are intelligent, good-natured and easily trained, and have been used as pack animals in this area since before Roman times. They are also surprisingly approachable: the photo below was taken from the Way through Simpson Ground – no telephoto lens needed.

Approachable fell ponies

3 Sedbergh

Sedbergh was the culmination of Friends Way 1 and it makes a fitting start of our Way. It is a town that is immersed in Quaker heritage. If you haven't already completed the Sedbergh Quaker Trail (SQT), we strongly recommend this circuit, which starts at St Andrew's Church.

St Andrew's Church, Sedbergh

It was in this churchyard that George Fox preached to a large crowd for many hours, making use of a yew tree that stands to this day. His message was so compelling that the Seekers present invited him to join their forthcoming Whitsun rally. The SQT also visits Fox's Pulpit – the inspiring location from which he delivered his Sermon on the Fell.

It was after this momentous week in June 1652 that Fox continued his journey, later ending at Swarthmoor Hall, where he met, and profoundly impressed, Margaret Fell: see page 16. Swarthmoor Hall became pivotal to the foundation of the Quaker movement, and it is deeply appropriate to begin our journey to it from Sedbergh.

The town sits at the foot of the Howgill Fells. The name Sedbergh (pronounced **sed**-ber) comes from the Old Norse for flat-topped hill. St Andrew's Church and Sedbergh's motte and bailey castle dominated the settlement in the 12th century. Its famous public (independent) school was established in 1525 and in recent times has become the town's largest employer.

Traditional industries were sheep farming and hand-knitting, and the town is a popular destination for walkers and other tourists. In 2006 Sedbergh reinvented itself as England's Book Town, joining Hay-on-Wye (Wales) and Wigtown (Scotland). For more about the town, visit ***www.sedbergh.org.uk***.

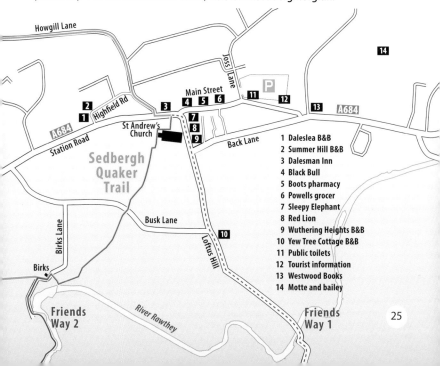

1 Daleslea B&B
2 Summer Hill B&B
3 Dalesman Inn
4 Black Bull
5 Boots pharmacy
6 Powells grocer
7 Sleepy Elephant
8 Red Lion
9 Wuthering Heights B&B
10 Yew Tree Cottage B&B
11 Public toilets
12 Tourist information
13 Westwood Books
14 Motte and bailey

3·1 The Sedbergh Quaker Trail

Distance	9·4 miles 15·1 km
Terrain	minor roads with a couple of very short main road sections, paved/grassy paths, stony and farm tracks; many stiles
Grade	mainly level with some moderate to steep undulations
Food and drink	Sedbergh (wide choice)
Summary	clockwise circuit linking several key Quaker sites, starting from Sedbergh and visiting Brigflatts, Fox's Pulpit and Drawell Cottage

This route is closely based (with permission) on the 2016 booklet The Sedbergh Quaker Trail: see page 70

```
0·0          1·3          2·3          1·5          2·3          2·0          9·4
 O────────────O────────────O────────────O────────────O────────────O────────────O
Sedbergh  2·1  Brigflatts  3·7  Lincoln's  2·4  Fox's Pulpit  3·7  Drawell  3·2  Sedbergh
                               Inn Bridge                        Cottage
```

- Facing the lych-gate of St Andrew's Church, walk 30 m to the right and take the paved path on your left down the outside of the church yard to Sedbergh School's sports fields.

- Turn right, and then left at a fingerpost 'Birks ½ mile'. Continue through the school grounds to a kissing-gate, and then down a grassy slope to a further gate onto Busk Lane.

- Cross the road directly and follow the gravel track signed 'Birks ⅓ mile'. As the track bears left at a broken wall junction, head straight on across the field until you reach a kissing-gate signed 'Birks'.

- Follow a clear path around the left side of Birks House until you reach a kissing-gate. Turn left onto the lane through Birks.

- Just after the double-bend in Birks pass through a kissing-gate in the hedge on your right with a fingerpost signed to Brigflatts. Ignore the sign to Toll Bar and instead cross the field, bearing left of the central rise, aiming for a stile between two gates.

- Cross the stile to follow a clear path at first alongside a wall, passing across the fields and through a series of taped-off horse paddocks. Aim for a small underpass on the dismantled Lune Valley railway line.

- Once through the underpass, cross the field ahead aiming for the large house (Rosebank) to the right of the whitewashed Brigflatts buildings.

- Pass through a couple of gates to reach a lane with the Quaker burial ground opposite. Turn left down the lane to the Brigflatts Friends Meetinghouse: see the panel on page 73. Even if the Meetinghouse is closed when you visit, you may find tranquillity in its lovely gardens.

West across the fields towards Brigflatts

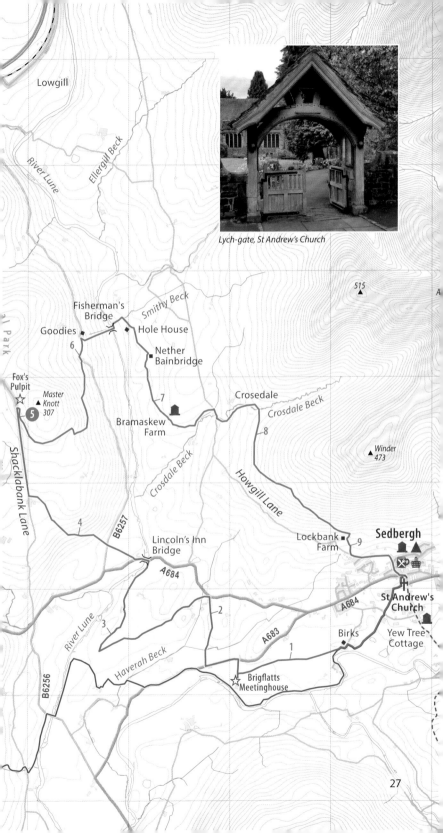

Lych-gate, St Andrew's Church

Lowgill

River Lune

Ellergill Beck

Smithy Beck

Fisherman's Bridge

Goodies

Hole House

6

Nether Bainbridge

Fox's Pulpit

Master Knott 307

5

Bramaskew Farm

7

Crosedale

Crosdale Beck

8

515

Winder 473

Shacklabank Lane

Crosdale Beck

Howgill Lane

Park

4

B6257

Lincoln's Inn Bridge

Lockbank Farm

9

Sedbergh

A684

River Lune

3

A684

St Andrew's Church

2

A683

Birks

Yew Tree Cottage

B6256

Haverah Beck

1

Brigflatts Meetinghouse

Brigflatts Meetinghouse

Brigflatts Meetinghouse, date plaque inset

Quakerism created an architectural legacy, albeit Quakers believe that worship does not require a special building. Fox preferred to preach outdoors in order to avoid 'steeplehouses' (traditional churches). However practical constraints soon meant that meetinghouses were needed. The hallmarks of a meetinghouse are simplicity, community and equality, with a total absence of traditional liturgical objects and symbols.

Brigflatts is a superb example, built in 1675 and with sympathetic restoration work done in 1900, 1977 and 2005. Fell and one of her daughters, along with Fox, attended a 500-strong meeting there in 1677. As the oldest meetinghouse in the north of England it attracts visitors from all over the world. Many of its original oak furnishings survive intact, and its simple benches and gallery make a tranquil space for Quakers to meet and share their faith. It is still in regular use by local Friends for their meetings, currently on Sunday mornings. Visit its website: **brigflatts.org**.

Interior of Brigflatts, from its gallery

- After Brigflatts go back up the lane (180 m) to reach the main road (A683). Cross over with care and turn left to face oncoming traffic. After 300 m turn right onto a bridleway signed 'Ingmire Back Lane'.

- The bridleway soon bears right at a field gate up a shady path between mature trees and an old stone wall. You almost reach the A684 road, but at mile 2·2 turn sharp left immediately onto a private lane signed 'Killington Bridge'.

- Cross the driveway access to the houses of Ingmire Court to a gate/stile and after another gate/stile follow the arrow on a fingerpost sending you half-right up the field past a waymarker post. Aim for the kissing-gate in the wall and go through it.

- Afterwards bear right to pass to the left of two clumps of trees and exit by the stile in the far right corner of the field, between two tall trees.

- Follow the yellow arrow to cross the next field diagonally, aiming for the right-hand end of the hedge.

Two tall trees at the far corner of the field

- Climb the stile at the corner and turn sharp right to follow the fence northward, having now rejoined the Dales Way at mile 2·8.

- Go through a farm gate and follow the track to another gate beside the track, now with a high hedge.

- The next gate takes you into Luneside Farm. After passing among its buildings, follow a fingerpost for Lincoln's Inn Bridge. Climb a stile, then be sure to turn left to follow the field edges until you reach another stile with a fingerpost on your left.

River Lune near Lincoln's Inn Bridge

Howgill Fells from near Luneside Farm

- Climb that stile and follow the path going north with the River Lune below and to your left. If you are seeking a rest, there's an attractive stone beach near the arches of Lincoln's Inn Bridge.

- Climb the stile at the bridge, then cross the busy A684 road with care. Turn left along the narrow road bridge to cross the River Lune.

- Leave the road (and the Dales Way) barely 100 m after the bridge at a fingerpost pointing over a wall. Bear left up the field edge, cross a ladder-stile and continue up to a taller ladder-stile that deposits you on the B6257: take care, its treads are uneven and it may be overgrown.

- Cross the road to a farm gate with fingerpost and go straight up towards fenced woodland. At the woodland edge turn left along the fence for about 100 m to reach a stile (to the right of the more obvious gate).

- Once across the stile, bear left to climb diagonally through the woodland to its top boundary fence, which you cross by another stile.

- Bear left to climb the hill ahead, with a line of trees to your right. One of them bears a waymarker disc directing you to bear right uphill towards three trees.
  Aim to leave all three to your right and look for two farm gates.

Ladder-stile to the B6257

- Pass through the rightmost gate and aim diagonally across the field up to its far corner and pass through the gateway. Cross the next field diagonally, aiming for the stile at its far corner.

- Cross the stile and turn left along the farm track and go through a gate to reach the minor road (Shacklabank Lane) at mile 4·4. Turn right to follow it generally uphill with some views of a crag called Master Knott on your right.

Gate leading to Fox's Pulpit

- After 900 m of road, reach a roadside conifer that marks the gate into the rocky outcrop of Fox's Pulpit. (Adjacent is a gate into the churchyard of the former chapel of Firbank Fell.)

On the morning of 13 June, a crowd of over 1000 had gathered, warmed up by Seekers Francis Howgill and John Audland. After everyone else had lunched, George Fox (who drank only some water) climbed the dramatic crag now known as Fox's Pulpit. With all eyes now turned on him, he preached fluently and passionately for three hours – demanding the end of the false church with its hireling priests, steeplehouses and tithes.

Fox's Pulpit

- The metal plaque commemorates Fox's Sermon on the Fell, and it's worth climbing above the rocky outcrop to enjoy the inspiring perspective from where he spoke.

- Afterwards, descend to its foot and facing the plaque, turn right along a fairly clear path through the rushes for 100 m. At a fork, take the upper path and follow it onto a sheep trod contouring Firbank Fell, with Master Knott to the south.

- Shortly a wall and track come in from your right, which you will soon join. When the wall turns sharp right, follow it downhill until you reach a holly tree at the point where the wall becomes a fence.

- Follow a track heading downhill and left, away from the fence, for 60 m until you join a good track which merges from the right.

The Howgills seen from descent to River Lune

River Lune from the footbridge

- Follow the track to the left as it gradually descends to fields. Pass through a gate and across two fields, then over a stile and down to reach the B6257 at mile 6.

- Turn left along the road for 200 m to a fingerpost at Goodies farmhouse, directing you to an old gate.

- Go through the gate and head straight downhill to a long footbridge over the River Lune, which you cross at mile 6·4.

- After the river, turn left for 50 m and then right beside a stream.

- After going 100 m upstream, turn right onto the Dales Way at a fingerpost and pass through the cobbled and covered way through Hole House.

Footbridge over the River Lune

- After the farmyard and three farm gates, head straight up and over the steep hill ahead, following the fingerpost to Nether Bainbridge. Once over the hill, take the right-hand farm gate and cross the field to Nether Bainbridge Farm.

- A fingerpost in the left corner of the field directs you to a small gate in the wall to the right. Go through and take the track to the right, then pass through three gates into a field.

- Continue to a stile and through a group of walls linked by a small barn. Head directly up the hill ahead, looking across the valley to see Firbank Chapel. It was rebuilt in this location after a storm damaged its predecessor near Fox's Pulpit.

- Still on the Dales Way, take the ladder-stile over the wall ahead and go on to Bramaskew Farm which is a working beef and sheep farm and offers B&B.

- Go over a gated stile in a wall and follow the farm access road ahead to a gate. Leave the Dales Way to head straight on towards several farm buildings, including a concrete garage.

- Pass to the left of the garage, down a grassy passage and then to a gate. Drawell Cottage is to your right, just after the barn: see panel and photo.

Drawell Cottage
Now part of Bramaskew Farm, this historic cottage belonged to the Blaykling family who hosted Fox in 1652. It was from here that Fox departed to preach on Firbank Fell on 13 June 1652. Now offered for self-catering, the cottage contains various Quaker publications and artefacts.
The barn was also the site of various events in Quaker history in 1665 and 1676. For cottage and farmhouse B&B phone 01539 621 529 or visit www.drawellcottage.co.uk.

- Just 20 m further on take the path through a wooden gate on the left. Head up to your left past a waymark, aiming for the rise ahead to a gate in the wall at the field corner. You are high above the small wooded valley made by Crosdale Beck.

- Keeping the fence to your right at first, head around the top of the valley. Go through a second gate, then over a stone step-stile. Exit onto

Drawell Cottage

Howgill Lane by a ladder-stile and turn right along the road. To continue the full circuit, leave Howgill Lane after 90 m at mile 7·5 and skip the next bullet.

- If you need a shortcut back to Sedbergh, instead stay on Howgill Lane, which forks left within 400 m to reach Sedbergh after a further 1·5 miles (2·4 km). Although the distance is only slightly shorter, this saves a climb and descent of about 80 m (260 feet) vertically.

- Otherwise, cross Crosdale Beck to reach a fingerpost and stile on the left. Go over the stile and follow the sign to Craggstone Wood up the steep hill ahead.

- Upon cresting the hill, follow the yellow-topped waymarker posts down to a fence above the beck.

- Then go up to two gates in the top left corner of the field. The ladder-stile and gate to the left lead up through woodland to two gates and onto the fell.

- Turn right and follow the wall line for

Entrance to the woodland

600 m up to its highest point. There is no distinct path, but stay roughly parallel to the wall until you eventually reach a gate in it with a track leading down to Howgill Lane.

- Continue past this gate and up to the next highest point of the wall where there is a further farm gate. From here, ignore the well-worn path uphill, and instead head off at an angle of 30° to the wall for about 50 m, aiming at a small tree on the skyline – almost due east.

- Then pick up a good track that bears right across open ground, crossing two streams and heading gradually downhill. Good views start to open out over Sedbergh and its surrounding fells and valleys as the track steepens and descends to Lockbank Farm at mile 9.

- Go through two gates into the farm, across the farmyard and onto a small access lane leading within 180 m to Howgill Lane.

- Turn left to follow the road for 600 m down to Sedbergh's Main Street, past the Dalesman Inn to St Andrew's Church.

3·2 Sedbergh to Crooklands

Distance 13·4 miles 21·6 km

Terrain tracks, historic bridleways, field/riverside paths, minor roads and lanes

Grade mainly level with some moderate undulations

Food and drink Sedbergh, Crooklands

Summary quiet, beautiful and scenic walking with breathtaking views of the Lakeland Fells, Howgill Fells and Yorkshire Dales

0·0	5·0		4·0		4·4	13·4
Sedbergh	8·0	Killington	6·5	Audlands Park	7·1	Crooklands

This route leaves Sedbergh to the south-west, and for its first 1·1 km shares a route with the Sedbergh Quaker Trail. After picking up a section of the waymarked Dales Way, it runs along unmarked paths, in places following the very track that George Fox would probably have used in 1652.

- Facing St Andrew's Church gateway, walk 30 m to the right and take the paved path on your left down the outside of the church yard to Sedbergh School's sports fields.

- Turn right, then after 100 m go left at a fingerpost 'Birks ½ mile'. Continue through the school grounds to a kissing-gate, and then down a grassy slope to a further gate onto Busk Lane.

- Cross the road directly and follow the gravel track signed 'Birks 1/3 mile'. As the track bears left at a broken wall junction, head straight on across the field until you reach a kissing-gate signed 'Birks'.

- Follow a clear path around the left side of Birks House until you reach a kissing-gate. Turn left onto the lane through the hamlet of Birks, now joined by the Dales Way.

- Just after the double-bend in Birks, the SQT heads for Brigflatts through a kissing-gate in the hedge on your right, but the Dales Way continues for 150 m on the lane down to JMP Food Services buildings.

- Here leave the lane on a footpath straight on, signed 'Dales Way A683 1 mile': see photo above. This path is well-trodden and continues along the bank of the River Rawthey through a mixture of woods and open meadows, through gates.

- At mile 1·5 the route crosses a disused railway line using flights of steps. Descend to the large meadow with an impressive iron viaduct on the left. Across the meadow to the right, look for the house at Brigflatts Farm in which George Fox stayed in 1652.

- Continue around the edge of the meadow which brings you closer to the house, but there is no direct access from here. Leave the meadow by a well-signed footpath that still follows the river bank and leads to a metal kissing-gate onto the verge of the A683.

Approaching the disused railway line

- Turn left and follow the verge path, then a 230 m section of road, before re-joining the verge path on the left for 150 m once it emerges.

- At mile 2·4, cross the road with care at a Dales Way marker and go through the wooden kissing-gate opposite, signed 'High Oaks ¼ m'.

- Follow the hedge on your right to Haverah Beck which you cross on a simple stone footbridge at mile 2·4. There are great views of the Howgills to your right, and the Yorkshire Dales behind.

- Pass through the wooden pedestrian gate, turn left and then follow the waymarker sending you uphill to the right of the rise ahead.

Path on the A683 verge

- Contour around and descend to pass through a large gap in the hedgerow ahead. Turn right and follow the line of the hedge to emerge onto the start of a hedge-lined lane to High Oaks.

Holme Knott from the path to High Oaks

- Follow Dales Way markers through two gates, past an impressive house dating from the late 17th century. Go through the remaining buildings to join a further hedge-lined track rising to the north-west.
- Within 200 m, pass through the wooden gate and turn left to follow a fairly clear path signed to Killington Bridge.
- After 130 m pass through a metal kissing-gate to a wooden five-bar gate, and onto a well-trodden path with the River Lune below to your right, through the woods.

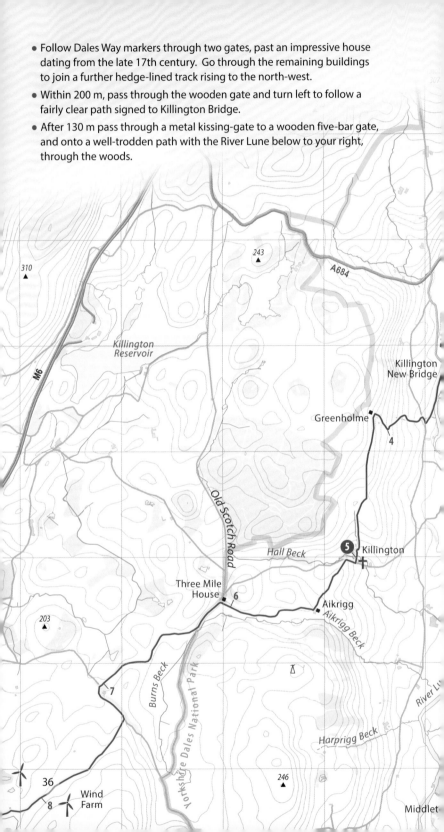

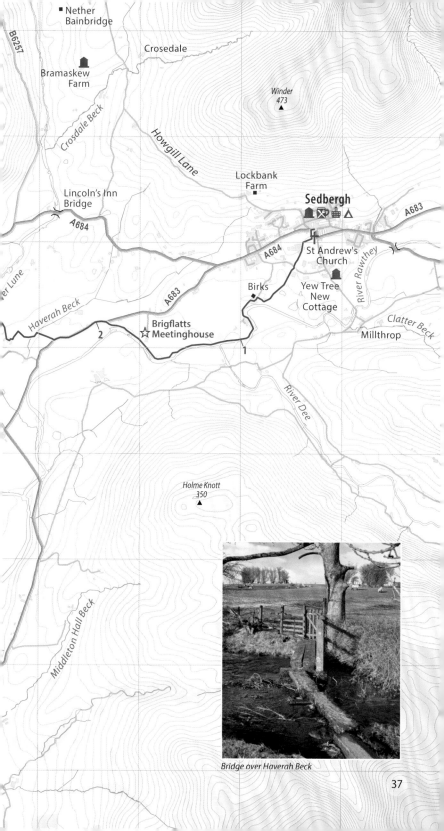

Nether
Bainbridge

Crosedale

B6257

Bramaskew
Farm

Crosdale Beck

Winder
473

Howgill Lane

Lockbank
Farm

Sedbergh

A683

Lincoln's Inn
Bridge

A684

A684

St Andrew's
Church

River Rawthey

River Lune

A683

Birks

Yew Tree
New
Cottage

Clatter Beck

Haverah Beck

2

☆ Brigflatts
Meetinghouse

1

Millthrop

River Dee

Holme Knott
350

Middleton Hall Beck

Bridge over Haverah Beck

- Continue on this path, perhaps pausing to sit on a bench to enjoy the river scenery. At mile 3·3 reach Killington New Bridge.

- Turn right to cross the bridge, and within 60 m turn left on the road signed for Killington. After 600 m turn right at the T-junction, but after 60 m leave the road by turning left across a cattle grid to follow the signed access track to 'Greenholme ½ml'.

- After 600 m of steady ascent, pass through Greenholme Farm, keeping the hedge and farmhouse on your left and the silver birch tree to your right. Pass through a wooden gate and ascend a steeper grassy track for 40 m to a fence corner, with an old stone gatepost bearing footpath discs on your left.

Killington New Bridge

- Turn left here and follow the fence to pass through a metal field gate with an old bath as a trough. Continue straight across the field and go through a gated stile. Beware of possible cattle in both fields.

- Continue alongside the wall to your right. Pause to enjoy wonderful views of the Howgill Fells and Yorkshire Dales.

- At the end of the wall, head due south between the pair of trees, aiming for a single tree beyond: see the photo opposite. Continue in this direction across the field for 400 m and descend to and through a metal five-bar gate.

View east above Killington

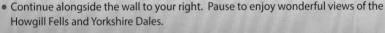

- After the gate, turn right to follow the fence line for 300 m and pass through a further metal five-bar gate. Continue down the hill alongside the fence, passing through a single wooden gate, and on down a small field – noting the footpath sign on the wooden fence to your right.

- At the bottom wall, pass through the small gate to your right into a private garden (still on a right of way), down some steps to the left and on to the access driveway ahead. Pass Killington Hall on your right (it offers Pele Tower self-catering, minimum 2 nights) and note the church on your left – well worth a visit if open.

- Reach the road at mile 5·1, turn right uphill for 100 m, then turn left through a kissing-gate with a fingerpost 'Aikrigg 1/3 ml'. Follow a faint path half right over the brow of the field to a stile in the hedge line.

Head between the pair of trees

- Over the stile, turn right along the field edge for 250 m and pass through a metal gate on your right. Now turn left and follow the drystone wall up through a redundant gateway to Aikrigg. Pass through a metal field gate, continue for 40 m and turn right onto a tarmac lane at mile 5·5.

- Follow the lane for almost 1 km to meet the Old Scotch Road at Three Mile House. It's strange to reflect on the era when the Old Scotch Road was the main route from western England to Scotland.

Three Mile House

- Turn left for 300 m to fork right on a minor road at the junction. Follow this for 1·2 km to a T-junction. Turn left, signed 'Old Town/KBY Lonsdale' and follow this road for 430 m, passing two metal field gates to your right.

- At the third field gate, with a dilapidated bridleway sign indicating Crosslands Farm, turn right offroad to join the ancient bridleway alongside the wall, one that George Fox must have used in 1652.

- Follow the clear track up the hill towards a small wind farm at mile 8. This offers wide panoramic views of the Lakeland Fells and mountains such as the Old Man of Coniston, Crinkle Crags, Bowfell and the Langdale Pikes to the right, with the Howgill Fells behind.

- Pass through a further field gate and continue ahead – this can be quite boggy at first. Shortly, go through a small wooden gate in the wall and head slightly right, around the gorse bushes, across a small stream, to continue towards the third wind turbine from the right. Where the track is waterlogged, make use of the ground to its side.

- At a short concrete post marking electricity cables, cross the wind farm service track and follow the track ahead down to a stream, then up to a field gate at a wall junction.

- Continue through the gate and follow the wall on your left, through a further field gate and onto a firm track. This now winds downhill to the B6254 road at Crosslands Farm, former home of John Audland. He was a prominent Seeker, greatly impressed by Fox and his Sermon on the Fell, and had invited him to stay afterwards.

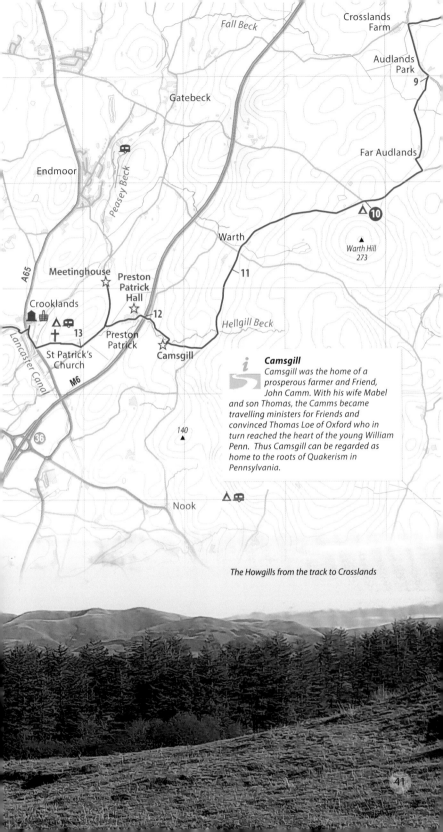

Crosslands Farm

Audlands Park

9

Fall Beck

Gatebeck

Far Audlands

Endmoor

Peasey Beck

Warth Hill
273

△10

Warth

A65

11

Meetinghouse

Preston Patrick Hall

☆

☆

12

Crooklands

☆

13

Hellgill Beck

Preston Patrick

St Patrick's Church

M6

Camsgill

☆

Lancaster Canal

36

i *Camsgill*

Camsgill was the home of a prosperous farmer and Friend, John Camm. With his wife Mabel and son Thomas, the Camms became travelling ministers for Friends and convinced Thomas Loe of Oxford who in turn reached the heart of the young William Penn. Thus Camsgill can be regarded as home to the roots of Quakerism in Pennsylvania.

140

Nook

△

The Howgills from the track to Crosslands

Bench near the highest point of the route

- Go through the double gate, turn left and head up the road to Audlands Farm at mile 9, on top of the hill. There is a good wide grass verge to use for safety.

- Pass the farm buildings then, opposite the entrance to Audlands Park, turn right through the field gate and head across the field, roughly parallel to the power lines, to a single wooden gate in a wall.

- Continue across the next field to the bend in a stream and cross with care at the ford. Turn left and head generally upstream to an old field gate in the wall. Enter a fenced lane – perhaps very muddy – leading to Far Audlands.

- Continue through a further five-bar gate onto a broad vehicle track to the farm. Pass straight on and up through Far Audlands, then left on the tarmac driveway to meet the road at mile 9·6.

- Turn right and go straight ahead on this road for a total of 3 km (ignoring a right turn to Gatebeck after 700 m) and going straight over a crossroads after 2 km.

- On the way, you pass Warth Hill Camping, with increasingly wide views opening up ahead. A convenient bench at mile 10 offers a viewpoint over Crooklands and Endmoor ahead. At 229 m (752 ft), this is the highest point of Friends Way 2.

- Descend to Warth, go over a stream and up to the crossroads. Head straight over and follow the road down to Hellgill Bridge to cross the beck after 800 m.

- Continue on the road for nearly 250 m, then turn right off it through a wide gate and follow the hedge line down towards Camsgill. Descend to and through a single wooden gate and go down the grassy, stony lane with Hellgill Beck to your right.

- Within 350 m, pass in front of the house on the grass at Camsgill: see the panel on page 41. Afterwards bend right onto the farm access lane, back over Hellgill Beck. Descend to meet a road at mile 11·9: turn left to pass under the M6 and arrive in Preston Patrick, with its Hall on the right.

Through a gate towards Camsgill

Preston Patrick Hall with Quaker Courtroom at upper right

Preston Patrick Hall is a late-14th-century house which was altered and extended during the 15th and 17th centuries. The upper room on the right of the building was used as a courtroom for the Court Baron. Several Quakers including Thomas Camm appeared there for non-payment of tithes – the unpopular tax whereby church or government demanded one-tenth of a person's annual income.

Preston Patrick itself was an ancient sacred place with a pre-Christian holy well claimed for the church and dedicated to St Gregory – hence St Gregory's Hill nearby. It was a priest-town before the Norman conquest and an abbey was sited there in the 12th century.

The old Church of England chapel became the home of the Westmorland Seekers, and the base for a monthly general meeting of Seekers including John Audland. George Fox attended one of these on 16 June 1652 as Audland's guest. The present church, St Patrick's, is built on the site of the former chapel, but still contains some artefacts from the time of Fox's visit.

- Continue along the lane for 250 m to a T-junction. Make a slight detour by turning right to reach the Friends Meetinghouse, still in weekly use, within 400 m. The current meetinghouse is a rebuild dating from about 1869. Access may be possible by asking at the attached cottage or website.

- Return to the T-junction and continue past it for 300 m to St Gregory's House. On the far side of the house, pass through a metal kissing-gate on the right and head uphill towards St Patrick's Church on the skyline. A section of the churchyard in the south-west corner has been set aside for reflection, with wonderful views.

- Leave the churchyard by a kissing-gate in its south-east corner and head down across the field to a narrow bridge over a stream. Take great care as you emerge onto the A65 main road, where you turn right to reach the Crooklands Hotel within 200 m.

St Patrick's Church

3·3 Crooklands to Kendal

Distance 8·3 miles 13·4 km

Terrain canal towpath, footpaths, minor roads and tarmac path through Kendal

Grade mainly level with slight ascent/descent on the Pony Path around Hincaster Tunnel

Food and drink Crooklands, Kendal

Summary quiet, beautiful, and scenic walking alongside the upper reaches of the Lancaster Canal and on its dried course with historic bridges still in place

13·4	4·2		4·1	21·7
Crooklands	6·8	Sedgwick	6·6	Kendal

This section follows the entire course of the northern reaches of the Lancaster Canal on its Towpath Trail, then crosses the River Kent to reach the Quaker Tapestry Museum. Its shorter length allows time to enjoy the museum and other features of Kendal.

- From the Crooklands Hotel, cross the A65 to the B6385 (signed to Milnthorpe), and cross the Lancaster Canal by a bridge. Bend right and, within 30 m turn right down the steps to the towpath, where you turn left.

- Follow the towpath under several bridges, eventually crossing the Stainton Aqueduct over Stainton Beck. After 2·9 km of towpath you reach Bridge 172 which marks the end of the navigable canal (mile 15·3).

- Continue for 700 m to a T-junction with Wellheads Lane. Turn left, following the fingerpost to Hincaster Tunnel and pass under the A590. Immediately turn right through a kissing-gate and go up on the Towpath Trail.

- Hincaster Tunnel comes into view shortly and you may wish to use its viewing platform. Afterwards climb the flight of stone steps to regain the Trail and continue on the Pony Path under the railway line and begin the descent to some houses on the northern outskirts of Hincaster village.

- Turn right at the footpath signed to Kendal and follow this down the side of the private property to join the towpath.

- Turn left and remain on the old towpath through a wooded area eventually emerging onto an unclassified road at a Towpath Trail sign 'Kendal 4½ miles'.

> **Lancaster Canal**
> The Lancaster Canal opened in 1797 and carried goods between Preston and Kendal, taking coal north and limestone south – hence its nickname, the Black and White Canal. Initially an isolated waterway, it was linked to the main network in 2002 by the Ribble Link. Following the lie of the land, it has no locks – the only canal of its kind on the network. North of Stainton it is now dry, although the bridges and course are still in place all the way into Kendal.

Bridge 167 over the (frozen) canal

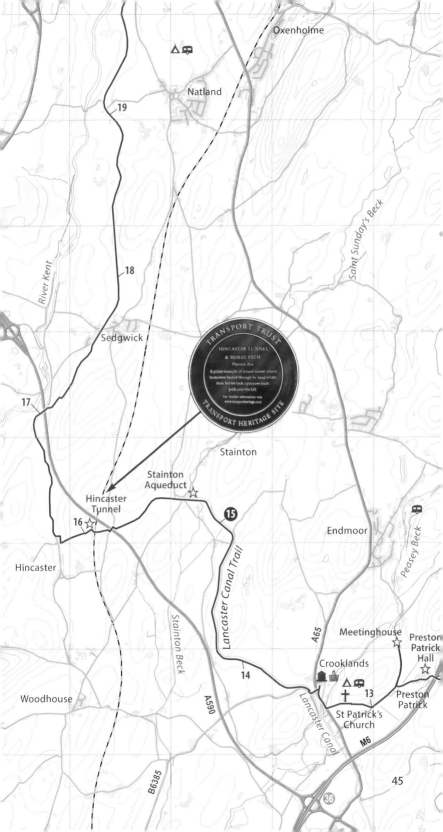

Oxenholme

Natland

19

18

River Kent

Sedgwick

Saint Sunday's Beck

17

TRANSPORT TRUST

HINCASTER TUNNEL
& HORSE PATH
Opened 1819

A prime example of a canal tunnel where
boats were hauled through by hand whilst
their horses took a purpose-built
path over the hill

For further information visit
www.transportheritage.com

TRANSPORT HERITAGE SITE

Stainton

Stainton
Aqueduct ☆

Hincaster
Tunnel

16 ☆

⑮

Endmoor

Peasey Beck

Hincaster

Lancaster Canal Trail

Stainton Beck

A65

Meetinghouse ☆

Preston
Patrick
Hall ☆

14

Crooklands
🏠🏭 ⛪ △🚐 13

Preston
Patrick

Woodhouse

A590

St Patrick's
Church

Lancaster Canal

M6

B6385

㊱

Lake District Fells from the Trail near Sedgwick

- Turn right and follow the road steadily downhill for nearly 700 m to a bridge over the A590.
- Cross the bridge and take the waymarked path to the right through a kissing-gate. Go steadily uphill on a well-defined trod path, keeping to the right of the field as it opens out. Head for the Dry Canal Bridge 177 ahead, with Sedgwick House to the left
- Pass under the bridge and perhaps pause on the convenient bench which overlooks Sedgwick House to the left and offers good views of the fells ahead.
- Continue along the towpath to cross a bridge over the road at Sedgwick and go straight on.
- Pass through a wooden gate, and later a metal one, to emerge onto a meadow. Follow the fence line on the left towards another dry canal bridge. The West Coast mainline railway, just to your right, may be audible.
- Continue through a further kissing-gate then under another dry canal bridge, and into the woods ahead staying on the well-defined path.
- On leaving the woods, notice a dry passing basin and Larkrigg Hall Dry Canal Bridge at mile 18·4.
- Cross the track to Larkrigg Hall Riding School, go through a kissing-gate and go straight on, following the left edge of the field.
- As the towpath bends to the right, you'll see views of a hill ('The Helm') and Natland Church to the right. Another relic of the canal era is the remains of a stone mooring post beside the towpath.
- At the next bridge, cross the stile under it and continue on the towpath. Another bridge comes into view shortly: pass under it through a kissing-gate and continue.
- After 400 m at a kissing-gate in a wall junction, the path becomes fenced and may be muddy. Within 550 m the path emerges onto Natland Road at a Towpath Trail post signed 'Kendal 1½ miles'.

Old mooring post on Tow Path near Natland

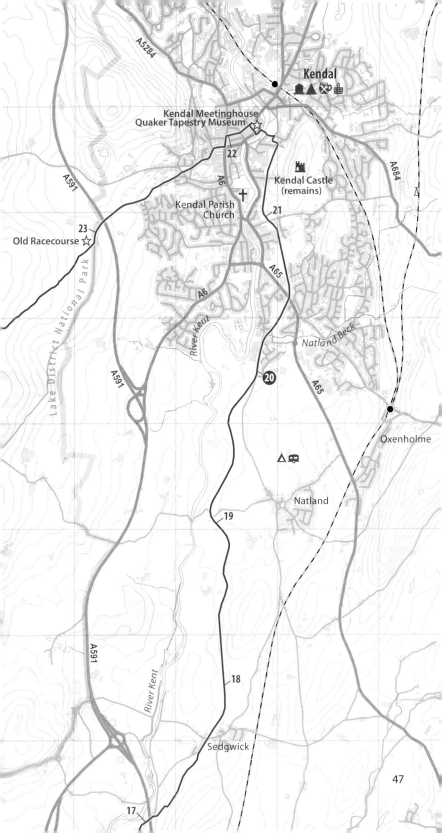

Kendal

Kendal Meetinghouse
Quaker Tapestry Museum

22

A6

Kendal Castle
(remains)

Kendal Parish
Church

21

A5284

A591

A684

23
Old Racecourse ☆

A65

A6

River Kent

Natland Beck

20

A591

Oxenholme

Natland

19

A591

River Kent

18

Sedgwick

47

17

Lake District National Park

Natland Hall Bridge

- After 50 m, cross the road and follow Trail signs on a tarmac path into Kendal, passing under a further dry canal bridge.

- Cross the A65 and continue on the tarmac path following signs for 'Canal Head North'. Pass the backs of Kendal Leisure Centre and Kirbie Kendal School and go on under Dry Canal Bridge 186.

- Reach Park Side Road and cross straight over. Pass under the next dry canal bridge and continue on a tarmac path, with a sign for Kendal Castle: for this detour, turn right and see page 49.

- The path ends at Kendal Recycling Centre. Cross Canal Head North and continue on the signed foot/cycle path on tarmac around the edge of a small park and then left onto Little Aynam towards the Gooseholme Bridge over the River Kent.

- Cross the bridge – installed in 2022 to replace the previous storm-damaged footbridge – to arrive opposite Kendal Meetinghouse. The entrance to the Quaker Tapestry Museum is at the far side of the building, beside the Garden Café. Visit from Wednesdays (Tuesdays in season) to Saturdays between 10.00 and 17.00. For a virtual tour and short video, visit *www.quaker-tapestry.co.uk*.

An embroidered panel created by the Quaker Tapestry project

Kendal

12

Kendal Castle (remains)

Kendal, formerly Kirkby Kendal, is a market town in South Lakeland and the third largest in the whole of the former county of Cumbria. Its population is over 28,000 – ten times the number that live in Sedbergh. It has become a centre for arts, culture and tourism, especially for visitors with outdoor interests, and Lakeland attracts many such people. Its website provides rich resources: visit-kendal.co.uk. There is also the Kendal Museum, beside the railway station, open Thursdays-Saturdays 09.30 to 16.30: *kendalmuseum.org.uk*.

Kendal's history dates back to a Roman settlement on the banks of the River Kent. You might visit the ruins of its stone castle, built in about 1200 on a whale-backed hill (a glacial drumlin) to replace the timber motte and bailey at Castle Howe on the west of River Kent. It was the barons' seat of power for two centuries, notably that of the Parr family. Katharine Parr (1512-48) was the sixth, and sole survivor, of Henry VIII's wives. After the death of her brother, Sir William Parr, in 1571, the castle declined into ruins. However it remains a popular destination in a commanding position over Kendal. Listen to the Castle Audio Trail here: *bit.ly/RR-castle*.

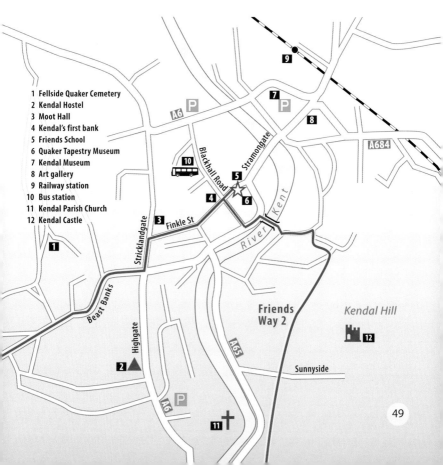

1 Fellside Quaker Cemetery
2 Kendal Hostel
3 Moot Hall
4 Kendal's first bank
5 Friends School
6 Quaker Tapestry Museum
7 Kendal Museum
8 Art gallery
9 Railway station
10 Bus station
11 Kendal Parish Church
12 Kendal Castle

Kendal Parish Church

The town hosts many fine churches, notably Kendal Parish Church. This unusually wide church has five aisles, each with its own distinctive character and history. Its nave dates from 1201 and it has a 13th-century chapel used by the Strickland family of Sizergh Castle. Visit also the 14th century Parr chapel which houses a fragment of an Anglican cross dating from AD 850. The church has superb stained glass and a wonderful black marble font dating from the 15th century: its website is at **kendalparishchurch.co.uk**.

From 1652 onwards the town has had a strong Quaker tradition, celebrated in a town centre walk that visits 15 Quaker sites. We recommend the 'discovery walk' booklet, available from the Quaker Tapestry Museum: see page 70. It gives details of the Friends School (founded in 1698 and closed in 1932), Kendal's first banks (dating from 1788), the Moot Hall where Fox preached in 1652 and the Fellside Quaker Cemetery (see page 51) – as well as 11 other Quaker-related sites.

Start exploring Kendal from the glorious Quaker Tapestry Museum, housed in the Quaker Meetinghouse since 1994. The 'tapestry' actually consists of narrative panels of embroidery, all 77 of which are reproduced in the *Pictorial Guide*: see page 70. Over 40 of these panels are on display here, along with 800 artefacts illustrating the Quaker history of the area. Displays feature prominent Quakers who set up respected businesses in banking, chocolate, shoes and brewing.

Each panel is 25x21 inches (63x53 cm) and their stories range from the 17th century to the present, including Quakerism, botany, science and medicine, commerce, pacifism and the industrial revolution. The 15-year project began in 1981 and involved more than 4000 men, women and children in 15 countries through embroidery workshops. The needlework uses a mixture of six stitches, including a Quaker stitch invented by Anne Wynn-Wilson, inspired by the 11th century Bayeux Tapestry. Known as 'crewel' embroidery, this ancient technique creates subtle beauty through its freehand flow and raised textures.

The map on page 49 illustrates further sites worth visiting, as well as showing how the Way traverses the south of Kendal. When you book accommodation, be sure to work out where best to leave and rejoin the Way.

3·4 Kendal to Newby Bridge

Distance 13·9 miles 22·4 km
Terrain tracks, historic bridleways and lanes, open fell, minor roads
Grade a steady climb at first followed by a steeper descent, otherwise mainly level with moderate undulations
Food and drink Kendal, Crosthwaite, Newby Bridge
Summary quiet, beautiful walking with the potential for breathtaking views of the Lakeland Fells, Howgill Fells, and Lyth and Winster Valleys

21·7		5·7		3·4		4·8		35·6
Kendal	9·2	**Crosthwaite Church**	5·5	**Cartmel Fell Church**	7·7	**Newby Bridge**		

This section follows footpaths and ancient bridleways offering some wonderful views of more distant scenery. In parts, it follows the tracks that George Fox would probably have used in 1652.

- With your back to the Tapestry Museum entrance on Stramongate, turn left and cross Blackhall Road at the designated crossing. Continue into the pedestrian zone on Finkle Street.

- At the 'Bandstand' (glass shelter) turn left onto Stricklandgate and head south to Kendal Town Hall. Turn right at the traffic lights into Allhallows Lane for 120 m.

Kendal Town Hall

- To visit the Fellside Quaker Cemetery (Kendal's earliest Quaker burial ground, now a public garden) make a short detour by turning right up Low Fellside. There are several historic gravestones, including three set into the wall beside the path. Retrace your steps afterwards.

- From Allhallows Lane bend left on Beast Banks (a former drove road to the marketplace) for a steady, at times steep, ascent. Follow signs to Brigsteer, ignoring any options to bear right, and after 250 m of Beast Banks bear left up Summer Hill/East View.

- After 130 m cross over Bankfield Road to follow Brigsteer Road uphill (mile 22·4). After 900 m you reach and cross the A591 dual carriageway by a bridge.

- After a further 230 m leave Brigsteer Road at a milestone and fingerpost, using a step-stile through the wall to the right (see photo) onto the Old Kendal Racecourse. You are about to climb over the southern shoulder of Scout Scar, a ridge ahead that rises to 235 m.

- Follow a well-defined track diagonally across the former racecourse to a gate in the stock fence and go up to a metal kissing-gate in the stone wall ahead. Take the stony path straight ahead which climbs steadily beside a fence.

The track up Scout Scar

- Where the fence turns sharply left, leave it to go straight ahead on a broad grassy track and pass through a metal kissing-gate in the wall.

- Continue straight on, always keeping to the stony track and, in due course, passing to the right of two bushy trees.

- The broad path winds and undulates before reaching a cairn and some ridgeline paths. The highest point in this section lies at about 215 m at mile 24·2. Continue straight over and descend a clear broad path to a larger cairn.

- Here, bear half-left and descend a broad grassy, stony track – not the ridgeline path which stays higher. The track narrows to a path and begins to descend sharply to a spur ahead.

- Ignoring all other tracks that contour Scout Scar, follow our path sharp right and downhill through the woods to a wooden field gate. In wet conditions, take care on this rocky path.

- Once through the gate, follow Footpath signs onto a track alongside a fence to your left and descend to the farm at Barrowfield.

- Continue on the vehicle track around to the left of the farm to pass through a metal gate and on to a T-junction of vehicle tracks. Here, a fingerpost under a tree indicates the path to 'Garth Row ¾ml': it goes half-right downhill across a stretch of grass to a wooden kissing-gate in the wall on your left.

- Through the gate, descend on part of ancient Garth Row Lane which is a bit rocky underfoot, and pass through a further wooden kissing-gate.

- Turn slightly left and cross the field to the stile in the wall and go into the woods. Follow a clear path through the woods. At a Y-junction bear left downhill.

- As the path emerges onto a forest vehicle track, bear right under the power line warning poles, and then bear left to a path into the woods between the overhead power lines and another warning pole.

- This path undulates and winds its way down to a wooden field gate at the edge of the woods.

- Pass through the gate and cross the field on a clear path to the corner of a fence with a fingerpost signed for Kendal back from the way you've just come.

- Turn right onto a straight grassy track to a gate and stile, and then pass houses to join their access track to Garth Row Lane at mile 25·2.

Tullithwaite Hall

- Turn left and after 30 m turn right between two stone walls to a field gate and small stile. Go into the field and follow the wall on your left to a gateway onto a track to the left. Follow this vehicle track for 350 m to another road. Turn right, immediately passing Tullithwaite Hall: see panel.

- Afterwards, continue along the road and after 500 m turn left along Grigg Hall Lane signed to Crosthwaite.

> ### Tullithwaite Hall
> Tullithwaite Hall where George Fox stayed on his way to Swarthmoor Hall in 1652. His host, Miles Bateman, had invited the local priest and many professors to meet his now notorious guest. The evening was marked by Fox refusing to eat, and 'a great deal of disputing'. However, Fox addressed a meeting in Underbarrow chapel the next day. The chapel was later replaced by the modern church, and most of Tullithwaite Hall was rebuilt in the 19th century.

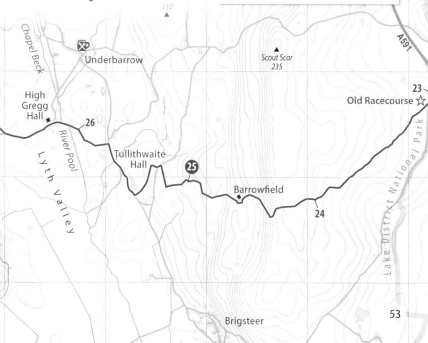

- After 650 m you reach a T-junction and turn left signed for Crosthwaite and Ulverston. Continue on this road (Blackbeck Brow) past High Gregg Hall (B&B and Lakeland Glamping).

- After 500 m on Blackbeck Brow, turn right on a signed footpath through a narrow stone gap and pedestrian gate. Head slightly uphill following the wall on your left, aiming for the white house at the top of the hill – Middle Blakebank.

- Leave the field via a gated stone step-stile, cross the next field to a gap in the stone wall, and continue following the left wall uphill to a gate into the garden of Middle Blakebank – rest assured, you are on a right of way.

- Head straight on across the lawn (passing in front of the house) and onto the access lane. After 150 m, continue and join Broom Lane, which is almost straight ahead.

Gate into Middle Blakebank

- After 100 m, just after a bend, turn right at the public footpath sign to go through the field gate and follow the clear path ahead. Go over the brow of the hill and descend to and through a small gate.

- Turn left onto the lane and descend to turn right onto Totter Bank, the road into Crosthwaite. Fox followed this road from Underbarrow to Crosthwaite, probably in the company of 'an old man, James Dickinson' with whom he stayed the night.

- Continue along Totter Bank for 500 m to reach the graveyard of St Mary's Church, Crosthwaite, next to the Punch Bowl Inn. The church and both its graveyards are well worth a visit.

- Take the path south-west out of the graveyard and follow its hedge-lined route for 450 m to reach Mill Lane. Continue ahead on the road past the Old Water Mill on your left. Cross the River Gilpin by a bridge at mile 27·8.

- After 80 m the road bends right, but you turn left on a track – aptly named Watery Lane as the centre can be a water course. Follow it for 200 m to reach the A5074 main road. Turn left to follow the road's verge for 160 m to the brow of the hill.

Crosthwaite Church and graveyard

- Taking great care, cross the road and head right up the tarmac lane and follow it for just over 300 m. After an S-bend look for the Footpath marker that turns you left through the right-hand of two field gates.

- Head uphill beside the fence line to the woods ahead of you. Leave the field and enter the woods by a wooden stile in the top right-hand corner of the field.

- The way is somewhat obstructed by fallen trees, but head left up to a stone stile that emerges onto an ancient byway that passes around Whitbarrow National Nature Reserve.

- Turn right to follow the byway, passing through a gate across it. After 600 m, turn sharp right downhill before a further gate, eventually to meet the road at mile 29 by an old lime kiln. There's a convenient bench from which to admire the Winster Valley ahead.

- Turn left onto the road and after 250 m turn right into the access lane signed for Broad Oak.

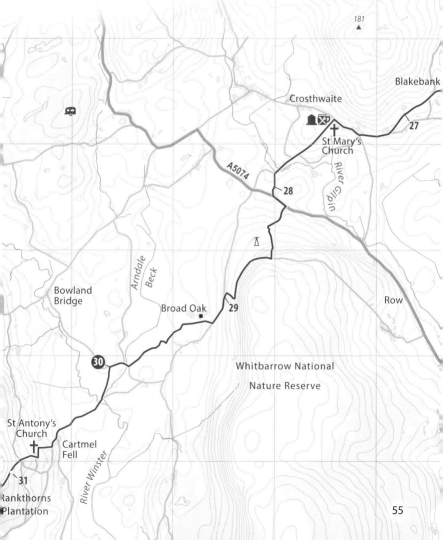

- After 80 m the lane bends right, but you leave it to go straight ahead through a single wooden gate. Follow the fence line at first, then cross the field diagonally and exit from its top right corner by another wooden gate.

- After 25 m turn left through a single gate in the wall, and turn left again once over the wall. Follow a path to a metal field gate and continue alongside the stream following Footpath waymarkers.

- Pass through a double metal gate and go on across the stream to a further gate by a tall tree.

- Turn right onto a broad grass track and continue on this waymarked route for 350 m. Pass through a metal field gate across the track and follow the fence on your right, past a short waymarker post on the left. Continue to a stone step-stile over the wall that leads you to a road at mile 29·9.

- Turn right on the road which crosses Arndale Beck and bears left. Within 180 m of the beck, turn off left through a gate at a Footpath fingerpost. Follow the path down the right-hand side of the field for 130 m and go through a stone gap-stile through the wall.

Approaching Lobby Bridge

- Head across the field, maintaining the same direction to a stone step-stile by the bridge with Arndale Beck once again converging from the left.

- Join another road at mile 30·2 and turn right along it to cross the River Winster at Lobby Bridge. Continue up into the hamlet of Cartmel Fell. About 600 m after Lobby Bridge, bear right uphill at a fork.

- After 80 m leave this road by turning right on a signed Foothpath that leads up through the woods towards Cartmel Fell Church: keep right on the footpath.

- Reach the top after 130 m and pass through a gap in the stone wall. Turn left onto a track to reach Cartmel Fell Church, passing a board about the wildlife and history of Hodge Hill.

- Leave the churchyard by stone steps and a gap-stile to the left (west) of the church's main entrance, and follow the wall up along the edge of the woods to emerge at a Y-junction of roads.

Cartmel Fell Church

- Cross straight over the roads to climb a wooden ladder-stile and then follow the footpath uphill to a stone step-stile over a wall. Continue straight ahead to contour on a clear path through bracken to reach and cross another ladder-stile over a wall into Rankthorns Plantation.

- Follow a fairly good path on the contour line, negotiating fallen trees as best you can. Continue on a clear path down through the woods to emerge over a stone gap-stile onto the bracken-covered open fell.

- Follow the path downhill. After a boggy stream crossing, go up onto a broad track at a short marker post.

- Turn right and follow the track through a wooden gate. Go up a walled lane to a further gate and fingerpost which sends you left to continue on a vehicle track. There may be views of the Howgills behind you.

- At the top of the lane, use the pedestrian gate to reach and turn left onto a tarmac lane which you follow down out of the woods. After 250 m, at the top of a slight rise, take the second track off to the right.

- Climb steadily for 170 m to reach and pass through a metal vehicle gate onto a walled ancient lane, and go out onto the open fell.

East from the vehicle track

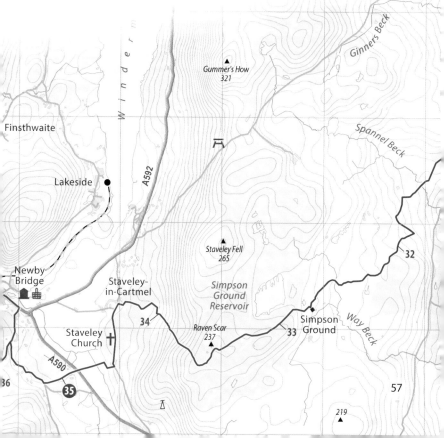

Bench with a view, Simpson Ground Allotment

- Continue on this track as it twists and undulates its way over Simpson Ground Allotment, passing through several gates and enjoying wide views from this lofty track. You may glimpse some of the resident fell ponies: see page 24. At a stream, use informal stepping stones to cross with care.

- After 1·2 km reach a fingerpost that turns you right alongside a deer fence, into the woods of Simpson Ground itself, climbing steadily.

- Turn left at the first junction, then follow the narrow twisting path through the woodland.

- After nearly 1 km the path emerges onto a forestry road. Turn left on it, as waymarked, for 180 m. Where the road bends left downhill, instead turn right onto a waymarked footpath, to re-enter the woods.

- Within 100 m bear right at a fork with a conifer in the middle, and head downhill. The track becomes increasingly steep and stony underfoot.

Stepping stones across a stream

- After 300 m, cross over a forest road onto a way-marked bridleway, and descend through old silver birch woods. Views of Lake Windermere appear ahead to the right.

- Descend to a wooden gate in a deer fence and pass through onto the open fell. Views of Coniston Old Man, Wetherlam, the Langdale Pikes and the Fairfield Horseshoe may be visible: see the photo below.

- Descend on a clear path to the woods ahead, possibly glimpsing more fell ponies on the way.

Coniston Fells from the deer fence gate, Langdale Pikes distant to the right

- As the path comes alongside a stream, pass through the waymarked gate in the wall and turn left onto an ancient track.

- Bear right at a gate signed 'Pigs in woods' and continue to descend. The track becomes the access road to houses.

- At the road, turn left for 300 m, heading for Staveley-in-Cartmel Church at the top of the rise (mile 34·6). On 20 June 1652 Fox had walked here to try to cap the minister's sermon with his own, but was forcibly ejected by a mob led by the church warden – and thrown over the churchyard wall.

Staveley-in-Cartmel Church

- Afterwards, turn right out of the lych-gate and follow the road for a further 170 m. Just past Chapel House take the signed Footpath to the right through an old black metal gate.

- Head down through the woods, across a bridge and over a black metal stile. Turn right to follow the black metal fence to the hedge ahead, over a further metal stile and then left downhill towards the A590.

- Pass through a wooden field gate, into a meadow and continue straight ahead over a simple stone bridge to reach a metal field gate at the busy road.

- Cross the A590 with great care to a wooden bridge directly opposite that leads to a gate into the field. Go through and follow the Footpath sign to leave the field by its top right corner via stone steps through a wall.

- Turn right on the access road for Newby Bridge Country Caravan Park and follow its main road down through the park. As it bends right at a refuse compound, head straight on up a narrow fenced path to the unclassified road at the top.

- Turn right and follow this road down to reach the A590 main road (and Lakes End Guest House) after 900 m. Turn left along the roadside path for 50 m, heading for the safe crossing point.

- After crossing with care, continue left into Newby Bridge which has several options for accommodation. Its name celebrates the picturesque bridge over the River Leven – a bridge that was being rebuilt when Fox crossed it in June 1652. At its southern end is a wooden bus shelter with useful visitor information.

Across Newby Bridge to the Swan Hotel

3·5 Newby Bridge to Swarthmoor Hall

Distance	13·4 miles 21·6 km
Terrain	footpaths, woodland tracks, historic bridleways and lanes, open fell, minor roads
Grade	mainly level with moderate undulations, but a steep climb up through the woods after Backbarrow
Food and drink	Newby Bridge, Bouth, Spark Bridge
Summary	quiet and scenic walking crossing the Rusland Valley with potential for wonderful views north to the Coniston Fells and south across Morecambe Bay

```
35·6              4·1              4·9              3·5         0·9      49·0
 ○─────────────────○────────────────○────────────────○──────────○────────○
Newby Bridge   6·6  Bouth      7·9      Broughton   5·6  Ulverston 1·5  Swarthmoor
                                         Beck
```

This section probably follows the route taken by George Fox on ancient bridleways, some of which have become modern roads. It includes many places that he is known to have visited, such as Colton Church.

- From your accommodation in Newby Bridge return to the A590's safe crossing point. Once across, retrace your steps to turn right at Lakes End Guest House and follow the road uphill.

- After 330 m, fork right onto a bridleway and follow this as it climbs for 600 m to pass through a field gate and straight onwards onto open fell.

- Pass to the right of an abandoned green vehicle on a well-trodden path and go on past two large holly bushes.

- Head straight on and slightly uphill to cross a junction with a larger track running left to right along the ridgeline of a rocky outcrop. Contour left and descend for 330 m on a fairly clear path that soon broadens over ground that can be quite boggy.

- Cross a stone step-stile over a wall that joins from the left. Follow the path alongside the wall to your right for 600 m as it gradually descends, providing views over Backbarrow and, in the distance, glimpse the Hoad Monument: see the panel on page 67.

- As the wall turns sharp right, cross the wooden stile and follow it downhill on a narrow fenced path. At the bottom, cross the step-stile and turn right on the residential road. You are passing through the southern part of the community of Backbarrow which has various options for accommodation. The settlement is somewhat divided by road, river and railway.

- After 50 m, turn left onto a tarmac path signed 'Lower Haverthwaite ½m' and descend to pass through a tunnel under the A590 at mile 37·1. At its end, bear left along the river bank to cross the footbridge over the River Leven.

Old Backbarrow

- Turn left then immediately right, up to a road. Turn right along it for 60 m and at the sign 'Lane Ends 1m' turn into Forresters Walk, bending right immediately towards the railway.

⚠ - After 60 m, cross the railway track with great care, and head left up through the woods on a good path – quite a stiff climb in places. At a path junction continue to follow the sign for Lane Ends.

- At mile 38, take the pedestrian gate through a deer fence signed 'Greenwood Trails' and begin the descent to Lane Ends along an ancient track between stone walls, passing through a further deer gate in due course. The stony, rocky path can be slippery especially in wet conditions.

- Reach the road to turn right, then right again past Lane Ends Farm. Bear left on the road to reach Lane Ends Road where you turn right.

- After 200 m, turn left on The Causeway, as used by George Fox, and follow it for 1·6 km to its end at the White Hart Inn at Bouth. Continue west along the road signed for Greenodd and Ulverston.

- After 250 m, turn right at a tree onto a path signed 'Public Way Colton 3/4 m' on tarmac at first, probably part of Fox's 1652 route. The stone track crosses a stream and climbs – steeply at first – into the woods.

Tree marking the right turn to Colton

- Continue to ascend, passing through a wooden gate and follow the broad track as it climbs out into open terrain with sheep grazing and scattered birch trees.

- After it levels out, and a 4x4 track converges from the right, continue straight down to Colton Church, which is well worth a visit: see the panel on page 62.

Descent to Colton Church

- Afterwards, turn left out of the church main gate and immediately fork right down a steep stone track which after 50 m passes St Cuthbert's Well on the left. This was used as a source of baptism water in the early years of this church.

- At mile 40·6 reach a road and turn left up it briefly. After 70 m fork right onto a Public Footpath 'Beckside ¼ m'. After a wooden gate, swing right downhill with a wall on your right and go through a waymarked pedestrian gate.

- Descend on a broad grassy path past a low yellow waymarker to a wooden kissing-gate. Emerge on the road at Beckside and turn left.

- Follow the road for nearly 500 m and then, at the top of a rise (mile 41·1), fork right onto Colton Hill Road.

- The road climbs gently for 600 m around the shoulder of Colton Hill. It then descends steeply all the way down to Spark Bridge where you turn right and cross the River Crake.

St Cuthbert's Well

> ### *i* *'Treacle' Bible at Colton Church*
> Colton Church was consecrated in 1578 by Archbishop Sandys of York. Together with another Archbishop he had commissioned a translation of the Bible in 1561 that became the basis of the King James version. Nicknamed the Treacle Bible, a copy is on display in a glass case near the back of the church. It lies open at Jeremiah 8.22 with the question 'Is there no tryacle in Gilead?': tryacle *was later amended to* balm. *George Fox used such a Bible and his own copy is on display at Swarthmoor Hall.*

The Farmer's Arms

- Continue straight on past the Royal Oak pub (temporarily closed in early 2023) and go uphill for 350 m to meet the A5092 at the Farmer's Arms. This historic pub was rescued by its local community in 2020 with funding from Grizedale Arts. It now acts as a rural hub – not only for food, drink and accomodation but also for workshops, events and local startups: *lakedistrictfarmersarms.com*.

- Turn left onto the pavement past some cottages, then cross the road with great care to a safe path on the verge leading towards the brow of the hill.

- At mile 42·1 turn right onto a road (Silver Lane) and head uphill past a converted stone chapel towards Wood End Farm, with widening views of the Coniston Fells appearing to the right.

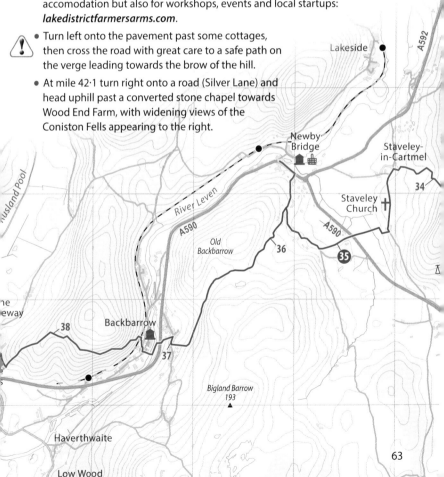

Coniston Fells from the Way near Summerhill

- Where the road bends right towards the farm, leave it to turn left through double metal gates on a farm track. Head across the fields just below the woods (Lads Head Plantation) on your right.

- After 400 m cross a waymarked stile and go around Summerhill Lake on your right. Go through a metal field gate and immediately turn right to pass in front of derelict barns. Follow the track to a wooden stile and field gate.

- Continue alongside Summerhill's walled garden for 100 m to a waymarker. Here bear right uphill across the hillside, heading for a clump of somewhat storm-damaged trees.

- Pass through or above the clump and head for a small metal kissing-gate. Continue uphill across a dip, aiming for the power lines to your right.

Storm-damaged trees

- Cross a small stream and where the power lines bear right, leave them to aim at a large oak tree ahead. Shortly, cross a wooden ladder-stile over a wall and head down through the buildings of High Scathwaite at mile 43·3.

- Bear left through the farm and follow the track to an unclassified road. Turn right and after 750 m turn right again at a T-junction.

- Follow the road downhill for 900 m to a T-junction. Cross the road to take the footpath opposite, crossing Moor House Beck by a stone footbridge.

- Follow the footpath for 100 m beside the stream. Cross a gap-stile and head left uphill to a gated gap-stile to the left of wooden power pylons.

- Turn right on the road into the hamlet of Broughton Beck, where you bear left, now on the Cumbria Way. Head uphill for 200 m to the junction with the B5281, where you turn left.

- After 120 m turn right onto an unclassified road signed 'St John's Church'. Reach the church within 400 m and notice the brightly coloured glass of its porch. The church also appears on our title page.

- Turn left at the Cumbria Way signpost and follow the track past the church and into the fields beyond. Head through a gate and on towards a group of three trees, then go through a field gate opening behind them.

- From the gate, bear left to contour the hill for 200 m on a broader trod path to a wooden kissing-gate onto a minor road at mile 45·4.

The track passes St John's Church

- Turn left along the road and after 300 m turn right onto the access lane to Hollowmire Cottage. Pass among the farm buildings and turn left after Hollowmire South, following the Cumbria Way sign. The path now follows a small stream on your right running around the field edge.

- After 200 m, cross the stream on a small footbridge and turn left following the wall to Stony Crag ahead. Pass through a gateway, and go around to the right of the buildings over a wooden stile.

- Take the signed footpath to your right through a wooden field gate and follow the wall on your left. As the wall bends left, head straight on over the fields to cross a stream descending from the right and then go over a wooden stile.

- Head through a metal field gate and up to a wall corner. Follow the power lines to a track between the walls.

- Continue diagonally right, again following the power lines to leave the field by a gateway ahead.

- Follow a footpath sign to the next gateway, where Ulverston comes into view. Join a vehicle track and descend to the road.

- Turn right up the road, climbing steeply for 170 m to Higher Lath Farm at mile 46·5.

Coniston Fells from the Way

- As the road bends left, resume the Cumbria Way by turning left on a marked path to Bortree Stile over a step-stile and across the field under power lines – aiming for the Hoad Monument: see the photo below.
- Cross a stone step-stile onto open access fell and bear right to follow a descending path that winds below the rocky outcrops. Where the path forks, bear right.
- Cross a wall at the bottom using a wooden stile and continue on the clear path across a grassy vehicle track.
- Head to a stone step-stile over a wall ahead, then cross a stream by a simple stone bridge. Follow the path down the right-hand side of the stream to pass through the rightmost of two wooden pedestrian gates.
- Continue through a further gate and descend the field beside the stream. As the path diverges from the stream, follow it to the right to a wooden stile and Cumbria Way marker post. Continue to descend on a well-defined path.
- At the bottom, pass through a stone gap-stile and cross the field to pass through two single metal gates and continue across the next field to pass over a stone step-stile in the right-hand corner.
- Turn right and follow the stream to a bridge ahead. Turn right again and head through Old Hall Farm buildings (mile 47·1).
- After the buildings, fork left onto a waymarked vehicle track between a wall and a fence. Where the tracks diverge, keep left (straightish) into a field with the wall to your right.
- Leave this field over a stream and wooden stile and continue on the waymarked path, again with a wall to your right. Continue over a further stile before reaching the road.
- At the Cumbria Way marker, use the stone steps and turn immediately left through a metal kissing-gate, then follow the walled path down through the woods to cross Gill Banks Beck at the bottom (mile 47·8).
- At the tarmac lane, head right, skirting around and below Ulverston Hospital grounds and follow The Gill down into the town centre.
- On entering Gill Car Park, pass the official start of the Cumbria Way with its spire of limestone, slate and red sandstone representing Cumbria's geology.
- Head down the right-hand side of the square past the Natural Health Centre and down through the No Entry signs along Upper Brook Street.

West over the Hoad Monument

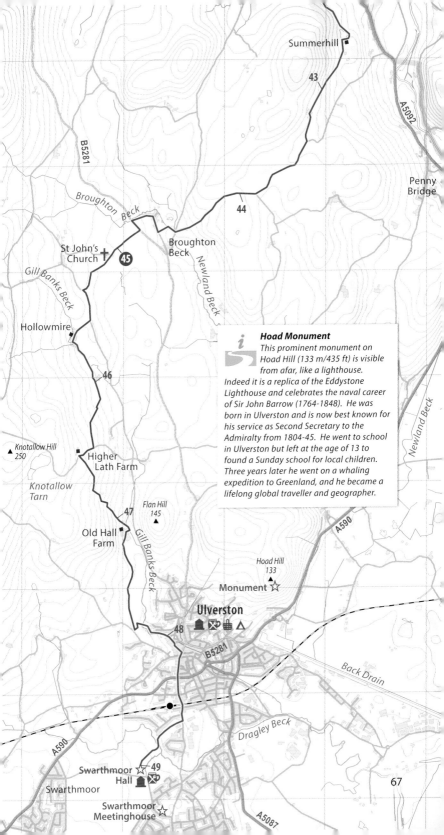

Summerhill

43

A5092

Penny
Bridge

B5281

Broughton Beck

44

Broughton
Beck

St John's
Church **45**

Gill Banks Beck

Newland Beck

Hollowmire

46

Newland Beck

▲ Knotallow Hill
250

Higher
Lath Farm

*Knotallow
Tarn*

47

Flan Hill ▲
145

Old Hall
Farm

Gill Banks Beck

A590

Hood Hill
133 ▲

Monument ☆

Ulverston
🔔 ✉️ 🏛️ △

48

B5281

Back Drain

A590

Dragley Beck

Swarthmoor ☆ **49**
Hall 🔔 ✉️

Swarthmoor

Swarthmoor ☆
Meetinghouse

A5087

_i_ **Hood Monument**
*This prominent monument on
Hood Hill (133 m/435 ft) is visible
from afar, like a lighthouse.
Indeed it is a replica of the Eddystone
Lighthouse and celebrates the naval career
of Sir John Barrow (1764-1848). He was
born in Ulverston and is now best known for
his service as Second Secretary to the
Admiralty from 1804-45. He went to school
in Ulverston but left at the age of 13 to
found a Sunday school for local children.
Three years later he went on a whaling
expedition to Greenland, and he became a
lifelong global traveller and geographer.*

67

At the High Street (B5281), decide whether to go straight to your accommodation (refer to the town plan below) or go directly to Swarthmoor Hall, in which case skip the next two paragraphs to follow further directions.

Ulverston is a historic market town with a population of 11,200, with a market charter dating back to 1280. Its canal opened in 1796 and brought prosperity to the town: it meant that ships no longer had to be beached on Morecambe Bay at low tide. Many warehouses were built and Ulverston's population doubled.

Back in Fell's time, travellers to Swarthmoor had to brave the quicksands, deep river channels and fast-moving tides of Morecambe Bay. In the mid-19th century, that changed with the arrival of the railways which relied on the construction of long viaducts over the treacherous tidal channels of the Rivers Kent and Leven. Ulverston is a dedicated Festival Town with many events throughout the year including a Walking Festival around April/May. The Visitor Information Point is in the Market Hall.

- Turn right at the B5281 with signs to the Railway and Bus Terminal and continue ahead on Queen St. Within 250 m reach the A590, and cross by the traffic lights. From Prince's Street head down past the railway station on your right and onto Springfield Road.

- Ignore the first right turn ('The Drive') but within 60 m turn right onto the signed footpath for Swarthmoor Hall which runs beside the grounds of St Mary's Primary School for 300 m.

- After the school grounds, descend through Kilner Park to cross a stream before a final 300 m steady climb brings you to your final destination – Swarthmoor Hall. **Congratulations on completing the Friends Way 2.**

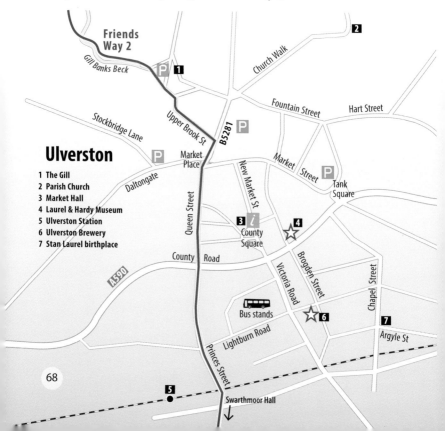

Friends Way 2

Gill Banks Beck

Church Walk

Fountain Street

Hart Street

Stockbridge Lane

Upper Brook St

B5281

Ulverston

Market Place

Market Street

Tank Square

1 The Gill
2 Parish Church
3 Market Hall
4 Laurel & Hardy Museum
5 Ulverston Station
6 Ulverston Brewery
7 Stan Laurel birthplace

Daltongate

New Market St

County Square

Queen Street

County Road

A590

Brogden Street

Victoria Road

Chapel Street

Bus stands

Lightburn Road

Argyle St

Princes Street

Swarthmoor Hall

Swarthmoor Hall

Swarthmoor Hall was built in about 1586 by the lawyer George Fell. He left it to his son Thomas, who lived there with his wife Margaret. After 1652 and Margaret 'convincement' by George Fox, it gradually became the centre of the Quaker movement. Meetings were held in its Great Hall until 1690 when the nearby Meetinghouse opened: see the panel below. Even after George Fox had married Margaret, his Quaker ministry and spells in prison meant that he spent little time at Swarthmoor. For Margaret, however, Swarthmoor was home for her entire adult life, including her final eleven years after George Fox had died in London. After her serene death at Swarthmoor in April 1702, she was buried at Sunbrick burial ground, a couple of miles to the south.

The Hall's Tudor structure survives largely intact, but it has been added to and subtracted from, its walls rendered, and rooms panelled. The building and its furnishings still evoke the Stewart era. The courtyard now hosts various modern facilities (café, gift shop, conference facilities) to complement the Grade II Listed Historic House, and there are three self-catering flats for 4-6 people, bookable via *www.cottages.com*. It is surrounded by peaceful grounds that make for a tranquil visit. Normally it offers a busy programme of courses and retreats. Visit its website *www.swarthmoorhall.co.uk*.

> ### Friends Meetinghouse, Swarthmoor
> *George Fox donated this site to local Friends in 1687/88, with instructions on turning it into a Meeetinghouse and some money for repairs. The building was adapted from the existing 16th century house and barn. The inscription **EXDONO:GF/1688** above the entrance proclaims it was given by George Fox in 1688, and it opened in 1690.*
>
> *Fox had realised that a dedicated Meetinghouse was needed and chose this site only 500 m from Swarthmoor Hall. This Grade II-listed building has been in continuous use as a Meetinghouse since 1702, as has its burial ground which replaced Sunbrick.*

In 1954 the Friends bought the Hall from a descendent of the Fells who had undertaken a lot of internal refurbishment. The Hall is now managed by a subsidiary of the Religious Society of Friends. As of early 2023 it was still closed as part of a three-year restoration and development project. This aims to make visits more relevant to modern visitors, as well as addressing the Friends' sustainability agenda. We are unable to do justice to the refreshed Swarthmoor Hall because work is still under way as we publish.

Two downstairs rooms are of particular interest: the Great Hall where Meetings were held and Judge Fell's Study, from which he would keep his door open and listen in to Meetings. Upstairs Thomas and Margaret's bedroom has fine fireplace carvings and George Fox's room features a 'travelling bed' (given him by Barbados Quakers), his personal Treacle Bible and his 1675 sea chest.

4 Reference

Further reading

Boulton, David and Anthea (1998) *In Fox's Footsteps: a journey through three centuries* Dales Historical Monographs 234 pp0-9511578-2-5 out of print but obtainable from libraries or, while stocks last, from the Sleepy Elephant in Sedbergh.

The Boultons' account of Fox's journey was the inspiration for our two guidebooks. They juxtapose Fox's route and life with the story of their 1994 walk in which they sought to replicate his journey. The book is full of thoughtful insights and highly recommended. Why our route differs from theirs is explained here: *bit.ly/FW1-FF*

Fox, George (1694) *The Journal* available as a 720-page PDF download from

www.friendslibrary.com/george-fox/journal

This version was divided into chapters, edited and annotated by William Armistead in 1852. It benefits from a long preface by William Penn and a helpful glossary.

Ross, Isabel (1984) *Margaret Fell: Mother of Quakerism* William Sessions 422 pp 0-9000657-83-9

Out of print but obtainable from libraries and specialist outlets; Ross is a descendant of Fell, and she also lived at Swarthmoor Hall for five years. Updated in 1984 (after Ross's death in 1864) by Milligan and Thomas this book is strong in its treatment of Fell's seven daughters who contributed so much to early Quakerism.

Smith, Dave (2016) *The Sedbergh Quaker Trail*

This 16-page booklet describes the circuit which we follow in 3·1. It is still available as a separate publication from the Sleepy Elephant in Sedbergh at £1.50.

Quaker Tapestry Musem (3rd ed 2021) *Quaker Tapestry Pictorial Guide* 89 pp 978-1-910514-07-8

Colourful and comprehensive guide that reproduces all 77 panels with explanatory comment, with a full A4 page to each panel.

The museum also publishes a 20-page *Souvenir Guide* to the tapestry and the useful *Kendal and the Quakers: a discovery walk* booklet by Patricia Hovey (2016) which guides you around the town centre.

Friends Way 1

Subtitled *George Fox's journey* this is the guidebook (2022) to the Friends Way route from Barley to Sedbergh: for full details, see

www.rucsacs.com/books/fw1

Useful websites

We maintain a list of relevant links on our website: please visit

www.rucsacs.com/route-links/fw2

to find many useful sites, including contacts for various places of interest along the Way.

National Parks websites

We recommend you visit the websites of the Yorkshire Dales and of the Lake District National Parks:

yorkshiredales.org.uk
lakedistrict.gov.uk

Accommodation

Both of the above sites have 'Where to stay' sections, and you may also find places to stay using *airbnb.co.uk*. Zooming in on our online route map (see page 71) will often reveal smaller B&Bs that are very close to the route. The site *visitcumbria.com* also has a good accommodation section.

Transport

For travel options from anywhere to anywhere, try *www.rome2rio.com*. There are airports at Manchester and Leeds/ Bradford:

www.manchesterairport.co.uk
www.leedsbradfordairport.co.uk

For journey planning and timetables within Britain, visit *www.traveline.info*

For buses to/from Sedbergh, visit
www.sedbergh.org.uk/travel/
getting-to-sedbergh-by-bus

For services from Woof's (Sedbergh to Kendal via Oxenholme) see
woofsofsedbergh.co.uk/?Service_Bus_Times

Stagecoach runs the useful X6 service which links Kendal to Ulverston via Newby Bridge. It runs hourly (2-hourly on Sundays):
bit.ly/RR-X6

DalesBus runs various possibly relevant services, but routes and timetables differ seasonally: visit
www.westerndalesbus.co.uk

Clear, large-scale mapping
Friends Way 1

Weather and daylight forecasts

The Met Office is the authoritative source on weather in Britain. Visit its website

www.metoffice.gov.uk

or download its app for mobile devices. When you need to know about cloud level, choose its **Specialist** forecasts tab, choose **Mountain** and click on the map.

For daylight and twilight hours anywhere in the world, up to 20 years ahead, visit **www.timeanddate.com/sun** and for this route search for Kendal.

Quakers in Britain

A comprehensive website is at **www.quaker.org.uk** with information about campaigns, events (including the Yearly Meeting), blogs and more, as well as letting you locate all Meetings in Britain by postcode. For the island of Ireland, visit **quakers-in-ireland.ie** instead.

Dates and calendars

In England during Fell's era, the Julian calendar was still in use: unlike our modern Gregorian calendar its year began on March 25 and ended on the following March 24, and it was also ten days behind. An added complication is that Quakers avoided the pagan Roman names for days and months, resulting in some confusion over dates.

When looking at graves, therefore, you may see dates that differ from those given inbooks and online.

Maps (printed and online) and GPX

Ordnance Survey Explorers are more detailed than our mapping at 1:25,000 and much of the route is shown on sheet OL7 *The English Lakes south-eastern area.* However for full coverage you would also need further sheets for the first 7 miles out of Sedbergh and (for the last 4·5 miles into Ulverston) the sheet OL6 to its west. For an accurate route map that you can zoom repeatedly for incredible detail, visit **rucsacs.com/books/fw2** and click the map graphic. The same page offers a GPX file for free download (under **Bonus Content**).

Notes for novices

For those who lack experience in long-distance walking, we have prepared notes on choosing and using gear. Visit our website

www.rucsacs.com

and scroll to the foot of page for *Notes for novices*.

Acknowledgements

We warmly thank Ben Pink Dandelion for his expertise and responsiveness to queries, as well as for the Foreword; and Carole Nelson of the Sleepy Elephant, Sedbergh who provided the original impetus and raised research funding; Meg Hill of Preston Patrick Meetinghouse who helped enthusiastically with route development and advised on wildlife; and Lindsay Merriman for painstaking proofreading.

Photo credits

Co-Curate p5; Robert Cutts p59u; Ward T Fell p16; Jan Fialkowski/*visitcumbria.com* p25; Tony Garofalo p13l; William Larkin p13u; Jacquetta Megarry p8 (four), p10 (four), p19, p24l, p28 (lower two), p29 (both), p30l, p31 (upper two), p53, p56u, p57, p58 (lower two), p61u, p62, p63, p64l, p65l, p69l; Caroline Mitchell p9u; Adrian Mullen p4; Quaker Tapestry Museum p17, p69u; Gordon Simm p21u, p22u; Dave Smith p33u; Peter Stott p30u; Whitewater Hotel p7.

We thank also *Dreamstime.com* with the following photographers: Neil Wraight title page; Mille19 p4, pp20-21; Philopenshaw pp 8-9, p66; Konstantinos A p20u; Dmitry Potashkin p22l (left); Philip Kieran p22l (right); Vaclav Sebek p23u; Ajay Kumar Singh p23l; Kevin Eaves p24u, p54 (foot); Bobbrooky p43; Khrizmo p49, p50, p56l; Chrisdorney p51u; Simonedge1108 p59l.

All 43 other photos not credited above are © Martin Budgett.

The well known engraving on p15 that may resemble Margaret Fell is of unknown origin; we don't claim to know what she looked like and we doubt if there is any reliable way of finding out.

Index